STEADFAST WITNESS
TO CHRIST

The **Voice**
of the **Martyrs**

with Lisa Anne Nichols

VOM
BOOKS

Egypt: Steadfast Witness to Christ

VOM Books
P.O. Box 443
Bartlesville, OK 74005-0443

ISBN 978-0-88264-148-5

Edited by Lynn Copeland

Cover design by Lookout Design

Cover creation, page design, and layout by Genesis Group

Printed in the United States of America

And the LORD said: "I have surely seen the oppression of My people who are in Egypt, and have heard their cry because of their taskmasters, for I know their sorrows."

—EXODUS 3:7

*"The Lord gave us this great example. He
was persecuted, and He told us in the world
He would suffer. But He made sure we knew
He overcame the world, so we are following
the same model. Persecution is part of our
faith, so we have to rejoice in what the Bible
told us is in our life. If persecution happens
in our life, then it is a privilege to us.
It means we are going the right way.
We couldn't see it before, but now I see
our trial the Lord allowed us to have.
This is strengthening our faith."*

—AKHOM, an Egyptian Christian shot four times
during an attack, March 8, 2011

EGYPT

CONTENTS

ACKNOWLEDGMENTS

Thank you to The Voice of the Martyrs for allowing me the great privilege of joining with them in their work through the writing of this book. Thank you to all the individuals at VOM and otherwise (including my husband, David) who looked over the drafts and offered suggestions for additions and improvements in order to create a product that would effectively summarize the history of the Christian church in Egypt and highlight the struggles of believers there. I enjoyed working on this project and learned a lot through it. I am extremely grateful to the Lord for giving me the opportunity to use my writing passion to help spread His Word, to bring attention to His people in Egypt, and to inspire believers around the world. I pray that this book honors the Lord and brings encouragement to its readers.

LISA ANNE NICHOLS

INTRODUCTION:
"I TRUST GOD BECAUSE HE IS ALIVE"

The devout Muslim young woman from Egypt was intrigued by her schoolmate's invitation to join her in listening to Christian radio broadcasts. This schoolmate, also a Muslim, enjoyed writing to the radio hosts, posing difficult questions she hoped would stump and trap them. Nineteen-year-old "Lana" (not her real name) decided to join in on this fun. She wrote a letter to one radio host explaining that she would never be moved away from her Islamic faith and challenging him to explain to her who Christ really was—whether just a messenger, the Son of God, or God Himself.

Much to Lana's surprise, instead of responding defensively, the radio host replied to her questions with a very loving, personal letter. She found herself strangely drawn to his words and frequently returned to the letter, reading it several times a day. In time, a friendship developed between Lana and this man who influenced and inspired her; she eventually met him in person and he gave her a Bible. Before long Lana surrendered her life to Christ.

When her Muslim family discovered that she had become a Christian, they were furious. She was now considered an infidel by her family. Her father, for the first time in Lana's life, brutally beat her. Lana was forbidden to eat with her other family members at mealtimes. Because they considered her unclean, they would not wash Lana's clothes with their own. Her family's anger soon escalated to the point that Lana's father threw her out of the house. She had been caught listening to a Christian radio program, and he could no longer tolerate this behavior. She pleaded with him, wondering where she was to go and what she was to do, but he responded by saying he no longer had a daughter. Lana was devastated. For several nights she wandered the streets, riding and sleeping on trains. Eventually she walked into a Christian bookstore seeking help and was given a job.

One day while she was working, a well-dressed customer came into the shop and asked for help. Lana feared no danger; after all, it was her job to help customers. The man deceived Lana into following him out to his truck parked along the street. Once there, he forcefully pushed her inside and drove off. The man was a security officer, and he took Lana to the National Security Office where he proceeded to interrogate and torture her for three days. She was beaten, her leg was broken, and her head was shaved. The floor was so filthy in her cell that she could hardly sit down. Terrified she would be raped, Lana cried out to the Lord. Despite her fear, when the man asked her why she would not cooperate she boldly responded, "You will understand once God removes the scales from your eyes." The angry man slammed her head against a wall, causing her to lose consciousness. When Lana awoke, she was back with her parents.

Over the course of time, her parents, in cooperation with the National Security Police, continually pressured Lana to return to Islam, but she refused. Concerned for her safety, she left home again on her own and went into hiding, eventually meeting and finding solidarity with other Christians who desired to share God's truth with others. Although she recognizes the danger posed to her life, she confidently asserts, "I trust God because He is alive."

Egyptian Christians praising God in church

Whether Copts[1] or Muslim-background believers, Christians in Egypt today, just like Lana, face persecution and discrimination rivaling that of the early church under the Roman Empire. Attacks, bombings, and shootings are frequent, as churches are burned, and homes and businesses destroyed. Christians are often kidnapped, sometimes by state security authorities. They are imprisoned or even institutionalized as "insane" and then intimidated, threatened, and tortured. Christian women are threatened with rape. Coptic girls disappear to be forcefully given in marriage to Muslims, and many other young women are coerced by their families to marry Muslim men. Christians who have converted from Islam especially are rejected by their families, reported to the authorities, and severely beaten or disfigured. Many Christians are killed for bearing the name of Christ, for daily living as faithful witnesses to the Lord, and for actively promoting the rights of Egyptian believers.

The plight of Christians in Egypt has a long and interesting history. Once considered an en-

---

1 The terms *Copt* and *Coptic* refer to the non-Arab native people of Egypt, deriving from the Greek word for Egyptian. *Copt* is often used interchangeably with the term *Egyptian* when speaking of the people of ancient or pre-Islamic Egypt. *Coptic* can also refer to the native language spoken by the Copts, which was a national language until the Arab invasion in the mid-seventh century.

tirely Christian nation populated by Coptic-speaking Egyptians, the nation today is populated mainly by Arabic-speaking Muslims who originally came from other Arab states. In Egypt today followers of Christ number about 10–13 percent of the population, most of those from Coptic backgrounds, the largest Christian community in the Middle East. Many others are identified as Muslim-background believers. There is debate regarding these statistics, as Christian leaders in Egypt believe that the percentage of Christians is much closer to 20–25 percent, with about 7 million being Muslims who come to Christ without telling anyone. Islam is the ruling political and religious force in Egypt, penetrating many areas of society and government, but it was not always so.

CHRISTIANITY COMES
TO EGYPT

Egypt had been an established nation for thousands of years before the first followers of Christ entered it. Because of Egypt's strategic location, its natural resources, and its unique ancient culture, the country has held a significant place in the shaping of world history, and God's people have played a prominent part in that history. In fact, stories of Egypt are peppered throughout biblical narrative and prophecy. As early as the twelfth chapter of Genesis, the patriarch Abraham and his wife, Sarah (then called Abram and Sarai), move temporarily to Egypt to avoid a famine. Later on, Joseph is sold into slavery and ends up in the land of Egypt, where he eventually becomes second-in-command to Pharaoh and is later joined there by his large, extended family.

Central to Christianity—as well as to the Jewish faith and heritage—is the story of the Exodus, when God sends Moses to lead the Israelites out of Egypt, the land of their slavery, into a new land of their own. God reminds His people of this great deed throughout Old Testament law, history, and prophecy in order that they might retain their faith and trust in Him. Egypt is also the topic of specific prophecies in books such as

Isaiah and Ezekiel. Last but not least, Joseph and Mary are warned by God that Herod is seeking to find and kill Jesus, so the couple takes the new-born Lord and flees to Egypt for the first few years of His life.

At the time of Christ there was a large Jewish presence in Egypt that had existed since the time of the Jewish exile and Diaspora in the sixth century BC. In the fourth century BC and afterward, many Jews settled in the port city of Alexandria, slowly evolving into a significant and influential minority. They were eventually absorbed into the Hellenistic or Greek-speaking culture of Alexandria, and it was there that the first Greek translation of the Hebrew Bible, called the *Septuagint* (also known as the Greek Old Testament), was completed. Because of the ease of communication and travel between Egypt and the Jewish homeland, it seemed a matter of course that followers of Christ should also find their way to Egypt.

Coptic Orthodox tradition proudly claims the author of the Gospel of Mark as the founder of Egypt's church. Though he was not one of the twelve disciples, Mark had a firsthand account of the ministry of Jesus, and his mother's home was a meeting place for the early church. Mark was the cousin of Barnabas (Colossians 4:10) and, according to Coptic tradition, he may also have been related to Peter's wife and therefore close to

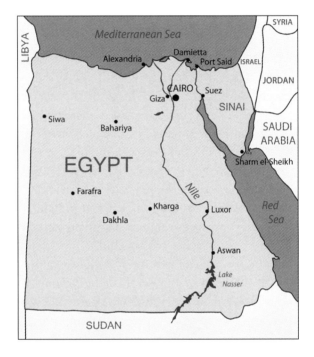

Peter himself. This tradition also states that Peter baptized Mark, and after Jesus' death and resurrection, Mark traveled with Peter as his disciple and interpreter. He was also a companion of Barnabas and Paul on their missionary journeys.

It is said that Mark was born in Egypt and returned there around AD 43. As he was walking along the road to Alexandria, his sandal strap broke, and he took it to a cobbler named Anianus to mend it. Anianus accidentally pierced his finger with the awl and cried out, "God is one!" Hoping that the man's exclamation suggested a monotheistic faith, Mark healed the cobbler's hand and preached the gospel to him. Anianus and his family were all converted to Christianity and baptized. More conversions followed in the wake of this, increasing into a significant Alexandrian Christian population. Before long, pagans who disapproved of this growing movement determined to stop Mark. Before they could harm him, he appointed Anianus as bishop of the church of Alexandria, along with several other deacons and leaders, and left Egypt, most likely to join Paul in Rome.

He eventually returned to Alexandria to visit the believers on other occasions, the last of which was in AD 68 (some sources say 62 or 64). During a pagan festival to the god Serapis, a mob of pagan worshipers, incensed at the vitality of the growing new church and fearing that Mark would lead it to violently oppose their pagan deities, decided to hunt him down. The mob forced its way into the church while Mark was leading a service and pulled him outside where they bound him and put a rope around his neck. He was dragged along the rough, cobblestone streets of the city as a means of torture then jailed for the night. The following day Mark was again dragged through the streets by a rope until his body became so mutilated that he died. Before his murderers could burn his corpse, a heavy rainstorm purportedly swept across the city, dispersing the crowd and giving the Christians a chance to retrieve the body and properly bury it. Today, the Coptic Orthodox Church in Egypt considers Mark to be the first in its long, unending line of patriarchs (often referred to as popes).

The message of Christ may have originally been brought to Alexandria from Jerusalem following Pentecost, as Acts chapter two states that Egyptians were among the Pentecost believers. Christianity in Egypt undoubtedly arose out of the large population of Jews already established there at the time. However, little is known of the first 150–175 years of early Christianity in Egypt. This may be because there was little distinction between Christians and Jews until the Jewish rebellion of AD 117 under Emperor Trajan. Under Roman rule, as Egypt was at the time, Christianity was not a legally recognized religion, which meant that believers had few to no rights, including the right to own property. Jewish Christians therefore assimilated closely with the Jews, at least ethnically, in order to gain protection from the ruling Roman Empire and to maintain their property rights.

Beginning in AD 115 in Cyrene and eventually spreading to Alexandria, Jews revolted against the

Roman Empire, destroying pagan temples devoted to Roman gods and attacking Greek and Roman citizens. These retaliated, and many on both sides were killed in the process. After this revolt of the Jews was crushed in AD 117, the Jewish population in Alexandria was nearly eliminated and Christianity slowly became more prominent.

Another reason little is known of early Egyptian Christianity may be due to the infiltration of Gnosticism into the early church. Especially in Alexandria, a melting pot of culture, religion, and philosophy where Jews, Greeks, and Egyptians had lived side-by-side for years, it is very likely that heresies and pagan beliefs from various sources leaked into Christian thought. In order to combat Gnosticism and establish a solid doctrinal foundation for biblical Christianity, the Catechetical School of Alexandria was founded around 180. This was a turning point for the faith, after which it developed a strong foothold. Through this school of learning, Christian theology was proclaimed and defended in a scholarly light. Two of the school's most influential leaders were Clement and Origen, both famous theologians and teachers who contributed to the shaping of Christian thought.

Clement of Alexandria (c. 150–215) was greatly influenced by the works of Philo, a well-known Jewish philosopher who had been a contemporary of Jesus and the apostles as well as an advocate of the Jewish community in Alexandria. Though the Gnostics emphasized the importance of knowledge, Clement believed that moral and spiritual growth should accompany knowledge, and he gave practical advice on how to live out a sincere Christian faith. Clement was head of the School of Alexandria from 200 to about 203, when he left for Cappadocia due to rising persecution. The emperor at that time, Septimius Severus, had forbidden conversions to either Christianity or Judaism, which resulted in exile, imprisonment, or death for Christ-followers.[2] Like most other Roman emperors, Severus opposed Christianity and disapproved of the Christians' refusal to cooperate in Caesar worship.

Clement was succeeded at the school soon after by Origen of Alexandria (c. 185–254), a teacher and interpreter of Scripture. When he departed the school in 230 to teach in Caesarea, he left behind a rich body of work, mostly about the Bible, that was instrumental in shaping early Egyptian Christianity.

---

2 It was during the reign of Septimius Severus that the well-known martyr Perpetua, a young noblewoman from Carthage (in modern-day Tunisia) in northern Africa, was executed in the arena for her Christian faith in 202 or 203.

STORY FROM HISTORY: ORIGEN

The teenaged Origen had just lost his father, Leonidas. The same persecution under Emperor Septimius Severus that had driven the famous Clement, head of the Catechetical School, away from Alexandria had also imprisoned and killed Origen's father in 202. Origen, wishing to follow his father's example, was ready to die for his faith as well. He wanted to rush out into the streets and boldly proclaim himself a Christian. His mother, however, stopped Origen from making such an impetuous decision; one day she hid all of his clothes to keep him from leaving the house. This seemed to have pacified the young man and brought reason to his agitated mind. He decided to stay at home and help take care of his family.

The bright young scholar was a student at the Catechetical School and had eagerly listened to the lectures of its famous teachers, Pantaenus and Clement, and learned by their examples. With such exceptional Christian role models as his father and these men, it seemed inevitable that Origen would follow in their footsteps. Soon after Clement left Alexandria, the young Origen, not yet twenty years old, succeeded Clement as head of the school in 204, where he worked for the next twenty-six years.

During his years as theologian and teacher at the Alexandrian school, Origen modeled and emphasized spiritual growth and discipline. He wrote many works for which he is still very well known. He was an interpreter of Scripture and is best known for his many biblical commentaries and books on theology, such as *Against Celsus* and *On First Principles*. He is also the creator of the *Hexapla*, a sixfold transcription of the *Tanakh*, or Hebrew Bible, and one of Christianity's major works of scholarship. This reference tool presented the Hebrew text of the Old Testament alongside variant Greek translations in parallel columns. To help him achieve all these written works, Origen employed several stenographers and scribes.

Origen hoped through his writings and his teaching to demonstrate Christianity's superiority over all other religions. He became so well known and loved that on at least one occasion, when visiting the Palestinian church, he was asked to preach though he was only a layman. The Palestinian church tried to get him ordained without going through the proper church authorities or rites in Alexandria. Because of this and other disagreements (some religious leaders saw Origen as too "bold" or "radical"), Bishop Demetrius of the Alexandrian church disapproved of Origen and came into conflict with him, ultimately driving him away from Alexandria to Caesarea where he opened a school and continued teaching and preaching.

Always committed and disciplined, Origen was ready and willing to die for his faith if it came to that. Just as he had earlier written to his father in prison encouraging him to remain steadfast, he encouraged his students to have the same frame of mind and dedication to Christ. He was sympathetic to persecuted brothers and sisters in Christ, and he aided and encouraged Christians in danger, visiting them in prison and sometimes even following them to their place of execution to uplift them with his presence. Origen himself also faced imprisonment and torture for his beliefs under the persecution of Emperor Decius in 250. Though he was eventually released and continued working, a few years later, at age sixty-nine, he died in Tyre as a result of weakness from his sustained tortures in prison.

Origen is still considered one of the greatest teachers and leaders of the Egyptian church, not only because of his biblical commentaries and exegeses, but because of the example of his life and death. In the end, Origen joined his father and the host of other martyrs at that time, who were strengthening the Christian church through their sacrifice.

CHRISTIANITY TAKES SHAPE:
THE RISE OF MONASTICISM

Christianity was firmly rooted in Egypt by the end of the second century. An organized church body with an authoritative head had been established in Alexandria, as had a reputable Christian school. But the Christian faith was not confined to Alexandria; it had slowly spread to other parts of Egypt, touching not only Jews but Egyptians as well. By the third century, bishoprics (where a bishop is in charge of each region) had been created and churches established all throughout Egypt, especially in towns and villages along the Nile Valley. Christianity was such a viable force that it had been recognized and viewed as a threat by the ruling Roman Empire, which took action against it in a series of periodic persecutions. However, this helped rather than hindered the expansion of the new church as believers grew more steadfast in their faith, desiring to follow the example of their crucified Lord. In 259 Emperor Gallienus issued an edict of tolerance, giving the church a welcome respite from the persecution and allowing it to thrive for a short time through renewed evangelization efforts.

But another factor would contribute significantly to the growth of the Christian faith in Egypt:

EGYPT

monasticism. Though the church was greatly expanding during this time, the message of the cross of Christ—one of gracious love, humility, and self-sacrifice—often fell between the cracks as some used Christianity merely as a means of personal gain. Within the church itself there existed competition among church leaders who desired to rise in position and power. Many churches were driven and dominated by those of higher social class, prestigious influence, and significant wealth. Because the second and third centuries saw periods of rest from Roman persecution, many self-proclaimed Christians grew comfortable in their faith, so much so that they failed to withstand the persecution when it did come again.

Because of this, many Christians came to view security and comfortable living (especially regarding wealth) as great temptations, and thus enemies of the church. These enemies caused church members to become too entrenched in worldly values and didn't prepare them to bear up under trials and temptations even to the point of death. For some, the solution was obvious: physical separation from society in order to put to death worldly passions and desires and to pursue a pure spiritual life. Believing that the body and the soul were severely at odds, that a person's soul (or spirit) could not live free or fully thrive if encumbered by the snares and passions of the body, many Christians began migrating to more solitary places to escape temptation and pursue a more ascetic life.

Though the concept of monasticism was not new, it was in Egypt in the late third century that it really took root and became an accepted, desirable way of life for the committed and disciplined Christian. In fact, two major Egyptian figures, Anthony and Pachomius, are generally credited with "creating" monasticism.

Anthony (or Antony), born around 250 to a wealthy family, is known for pioneering the solitary way of monks. As a young man, he felt compelled to follow Jesus' command to the rich man in Mark 10:21 to sell everything he owned, give it to the poor, and follow Jesus. In 270, after his parents died, Anthony made provision for his sister, gave away his wealth, and then set out into the desert to pursue an ascetic life, characterized by solitude and self-denial in a demonstration against worldliness and materialism. Others heard of him and eventually followed, some visiting him for healing or guidance, some desiring to learn from his example. Many actually followed his lead and began residing in nearby caves. In this way, Anthony became a well-known teacher and gathered disciples. By 305 he had given up his solitary life and had begun to live together in community with his followers. He developed codes of conduct, and from his example more monasteries and hermitages sprang up in the wilderness of Egypt, some founded by Anthony himself. They became small desert settlements composed of Christians dedicated to spiritual discipline and study. Each monastery was fitted with a church, a dining hall, personal dwellings for the monks, and workshops or storehouses where the monks created products that they sold in the towns and cities for their subsistence. Female monks, or nuns, also had separate hermitages dedicated to the same purposes as the men.

Pachomius, born around 290, joined one of these monasteries and later, in 323, founded his own monastic community in Upper Egypt based on Anthony's model, but with slight differences in its organization and structure. He ultimately established nine monasteries for men and two for women. By the year 400, numerous monasteries had been founded all over Egypt housing thousands of monks.

Though Anthony and Pachomius had chosen the monk's lifestyle out of a sense of spiritual desire and duty, some who chose that way of life did so as a result of persecution, especially after 303. In that year, Emperor Diocletian had recalled the edict of tolerance, ending four decades of peace, and beginning what later came to be called the "Great Persecution" under his reign. Diocle-

tian wanted to restore the former glory of Rome
and honor the old gods. He therefore set out to
eradicate Christianity by having churches destroyed, Christian texts confiscated, pagan sacrifices ordered, and Christians murdered. Many
hundreds of Egyptian Christians were martyred
during this time; in fact, so infamous was this
persecution that the Coptic Christian church dates
its calendar based on the first year of Diocletian's
reign, AD 284, which to the Copts is 1 AM (*anno
martyrium*). Because of this persecution, many
Christians fled to the desert and sought refuge in
the monastic communities that were developing
there. Anthony is known to have gone into the
cities to visit imprisoned Christians and offer
them comfort and spiritual guidance. Sources say
that he may even have accompanied many of them
to their executions, supporting and empowering
them in their last minutes on earth.

As Christianity grew and flourished in these
dedicated and devout communities, the old pagan
religions of Egypt began to decline drastically.
But aside from encouraging an authentic practice
of the Christian faith, monasticism was also instrumental in establishing a form of Christianity
that was more national Coptic and less Hellenistic.
Monks were almost primarily responsible for
translating works from Greek into Coptic, the
native language of the Egyptians, and by the third

century portions of the Bible and other Christian writings were made available in Coptic. The monastic movement thus helped spread the use of Coptic so that it became more of a national language, especially among the Copts, who were at this point primarily Christian. And as we shall see later, the monasteries of Egypt were also influential in strengthening and preserving Christianity in the Middle Ages.

STORIES FROM HISTORY: FAITHFUL WITNESSES UNDER DIOCLETIAN'S REIGN

Theban Legion

In September 286, thousands of faithful believers from the city of Thebes in Upper Egypt were cruelly killed for their allegiance to Christ. With Egypt having been absorbed into the Roman Empire, a multitude of Egyptian men called the Theban Legion served in the emperor's army. Though as military men they shared a loyalty to the empire, as Christians their first loyalty was to Christ. The Theban Legion was well respected for its good service, and its reputation spread far. When Maximian, second-in-command to Emperor Diocletian, was tasked with appointing soldiers to quell a rebellion in Gaul and bring order to the province, he chose to send the Theban Legion.

Around 6,600 Christian soldiers from Egypt made the long journey to Europe and prepared for their military campaign against Gaul under orders from Maximian, who had been bestowed with the title of Caesar. From there, a couple different things may have happened according to variant stories. It may have been that their campaign was successful, and that in order to celebrate Maximian ordered all his troops to take the Oath of Allegiance (with its not-so-subtle suggestion that Maximian, like other Roman emperors, was a deity) and then to eradicate all Christian civilians left in the area. It could also be that on the eve of battle, Maximian went into a pagan temple to make sacrifices and seek favor from his gods, and ordered his soldiers to do so likewise. Perhaps what angered Maximian against the Theban Legion was a combination of both commands. Either way, the men of the legion refused to comply with his order, as to do so would violate their Christian beliefs and their first loyalty to God. When they communicated this to him, Maximian grew furious and tried to intimidate them into compliance. He thus ordered a decimation of the legion, in which every tenth man was put to death. This having been carried out successfully, he expected that the remaining soldiers would now obey his orders, but they didn't. Even the legion's commander remained steadfast and stood up to Maximian, refusing to bow down to false gods or to kill innocent civilians and fellow believers. The survivors of the decimation banded together and composed a letter to him:

> Great Caesar, we are your soldiers, and at the same time we are God's slaves. We owe you our military service, but our

prime allegiance we owe to God. From you we receive our daily wages; from Him our eternal reward. Great Caesar, we cannot obey any order if it runs counter to God's commands. If your orders coincide with God's commands we will certainly obey them; if not, we ought to obey God rather than men, for our loyalty to Him surpasses all other loyalties. We are not rebels; if we were, we would defend ourselves for we have our weapons. But we prefer to die upright than to live stained. As Christians we will serve you. But we will not relinquish our faith in our Lord, and this we openly declare.

*"But Peter and the other apostles
answered and said:
'We ought to obey God rather than men.'"*
—ACTS 5:29

Maximian then ordered a second decimation, and hundreds more of the faithful Egyptian soldiers were slaughtered. Still the Christians would not budge, choosing to honor their true Lord over honoring Maximian. In a rage, the man condemned the remaining legion and had the Roman soldiers massacre them. Though the men of the Theban Legion had been good, faithful, highly reputable soldiers in service to the emperor, he ultimately turned against them because they chose to honor their Lord in heaven over a false god on earth.

Demiana

Demiana was an only child raised in a pious Christian home in the Nile Delta area in Egypt. Her father, Marcus, was the governor of the Borollos district, and he and his wife taught their daughter to fear and love the Lord. Demiana was a student of the Scriptures, and from an early age she spent much time poring over them. When she was of an age to be married her parents spoke with her on the subject, but Demiana was not interested in marriage or the distractions and priorities that came with it. Her whole heart's desire was to continue studying God's Word and to dedicate her life in service to Him. She asked her father if, instead of marrying, she might be given a safe, secluded place to live with her friends of a similar mind, where they might dedicate their lives in service and worship to the Lord. Her father agreed and built her a large mansion in Zaafaran where Demiana lived with forty other Christian women in a kind of convent or nunnery.

Some time later, the emperor, Diocletian, presumably on a visit to Egypt, asked the Egyptian nobleman to worship with him at a pagan temple in honor of the Roman gods. Marcus was among those invited, and though he might have hesitated at first, he ended up complying with the emperor's order, perhaps out of fear for his life. He accompanied many others in worshiping at the pagan temple, keeping quiet about his Christian faith.

Later, when Demiana heard what had happened, she was heartbroken at her father's actions. She left her mansion and went into the city to visit with her father. She broke into tears and lamentations as her father rushed forward to greet her, scolding him soundly for meekly obeying the emperor instead of having the fortitude to defend the Christian faith. She told her father she would rather have seen him killed for confessing Christ than continue to live having denied Him and given in to the emperor out of fear. Marcus was so moved by his daughter's words that he promised to right his wrong.

Marcus soon went to see the emperor again, this time humbly confessing his faith in Christ. Angry to learn that Marcus was a Christian, Diocletian attempted to persuade him from his faith but was unsuccessful. He then ordered Marcus to be beheaded.

When Diocletian later heard that Marcus's daughter was also a Christian and was responsible for encouraging her father to stand up for his faith, he sent soldiers to her mansion to persuade her away from Christianity. Demiana firmly stood her ground and defended her belief in the one true God, saying, "The Lord Christ I confess, on Him I rely, in His name I die, and through Him I live forever." She and her forty companions were then taken away and tortured, such tortures that may have included a squeezing press and boiling oil. Diocletian's efforts to convince them to denounce their Lord were unsuccessful. All the women remained steadfast and continued praising the Lord. In the end they were all beheaded and joined with the many others before and after them who would earn the title of martyr.

Mena
By the time Mena was just a young teenager, both his parents had died, leaving him an orphan. His father had been a respected and well-liked governor of an Egyptian province near Alexandria. Both Mena's parents were Christians and had raised him in a God-fearing Christian home. Because of his character and integrity, Mena also earned the esteem of the people just as his father had. Soon after his parents' deaths, he joined the Roman army for a few years, and sources say that he may also have followed in his father's footsteps by becoming governor after him.

About that time, Emperor Diocletian began his persecution of Christians, and Mena subsequently retired from his high position to seek solace and safety in the desert after the fashion of the monks. There he lived in solitude, worshiping the Lord through prayer and fasting. One day, though, he experienced a vision in which the heavens were opened and Mena saw Christian martyrs being crowned with beautiful crowns of martyrdom. This vision convicted him; perhaps he felt that he was not fully serving the Lord by hiding away in the desert. Whatever his motivation, Mena was compelled to return to Alexandria and declare openly that he was a follower of Jesus Christ.

Learning that Mena was a Christian, the Roman governor tried to dissuade Mena from his faith. He liked Mena and knew that he was from a noble family. He bribed him with gifts and favors if he would only turn away from Christianity. When this gentle persuasion didn't work, the governor turned to threats and torture. Mena bore these all without wavering in his decision to be a faithful witness of the Lord, even to death. In the end he was beheaded for his steadfast commitment to Christ.

CHRISTIANITY TAKES SHAPE: THE COUNCILS

Though persecution of Christians in Egypt had reached a pinnacle in 303 under Emperor Diocletian, Christianity continued to thrive and grow, especially due to the influence of monasticism. Before long, however, Christianity throughout the entire Roman Empire won a great victory in 313 when Emperor Constantine legalized Christianity and granted freedom of worship to all Christians. Shortly afterward, he established a new capital city in the east named after himself—Constantinople in modern-day Turkey—and Egypt became part of the Eastern Roman (or Byzantine) Empire.

In time Christianity became the official state religion. The Egyptian church was no longer restricted, and it soon grew into one of the major recognized Christian churches in the empire. The Alexandrian patriarchs, church bishops (who were increasingly chosen from among the population of monks), and other influential Egyptian church leaders played significant roles in several ecumenical councils that occurred during the fourth and fifth centuries, making Egypt one of the leaders of the Christian world at the time. The purpose of the councils was to unify Christian belief by addressing certain heretical teachings that were infiltrating the church, and to come to an agreement on basic and universal biblical truth and doctrine.

The first was the council of Nicaea in 325, summoned by Emperor Constantine himself, during which the famous Nicene Creed was developed. This council came as a result of one of the first major disputes to hit the church of Alexandria: the Arian controversy. It began around 318 with a man named Arius, a church elder and theologian in Alexandria who challenged the established beliefs that Christ was the Word of God made flesh, that God the Father and Jesus Christ were of the same substance, and that Jesus was both human and divine. Arius came into conflict with Bishop Alexander on this issue, asserting that God was separate, uncreated, and unknowable while Jesus Christ was created, and therefore did not always exist and was not eternally equal with God. Arius's beliefs, which came to be known as Arianism, were largely rejected by Alexandria and Egypt, but gained popularity among some Christians outside of Egypt.

Because of continued debates and growing agitation caused by this controversy, Emperor Constantine in 325 summoned the council of Nicaea, composed of over three hundred representatives of the church from differing nations, mostly Eastern bishops. Arianism was promptly rejected by the council as a heresy, and the Nicene Creed was drawn up to declare the church's official position on the Trinity. One of the three authors of the Creed was the Egyptian Athanasius, who was at Nicaea as Bishop Alexander's archdeacon, but later become bishop himself and then patriarch of Alexandria. Throughout his life, Athanasius was an uncompromising supporter of the Nicene Creed. Christian churches today still cite the Nicene Creed as a foundational statement of doctrinal truth.

In 381, another council at Constantinople, the eastern "Rome," confirmed the Nicene Creed and also made a few additions to one of its clauses, finally ending the strong sway of Arianism. However, other issues spawned by this controversy and regarding the nature of Christ trickled down throughout the years, eventually gaining force. A third major council occurred in Ephesus in 431 (followed by another smaller council in Ephesus in 449) to try to settle the issue of how a divine Jesus, equal with God the Father, can also be human. Egypt was a major player in these councils, with the Alexandrian church considered second to Rome in ecclesiastical authority. The fourth major council at Chalcedon in 451 changed all of that.

The council at Chalcedon was the result of continuing theological controversies and quarrels over the nature of Christ, in which the Roman church, including Constantinople, took a separate position from Alexandria. A schism developed largely based on misunderstandings over terminology, but was aided by cultural and political issues between the churches. Disagreement continued for years even beyond the council itself (especially during the years 540–578), the outcome of which was that Constantinople displaced Alexandria by becoming second in status to Rome. Two Egyptian churches emerged by the middle of the sixth century as a result of the Chalcedonian controversy: the Melchite or "royal" church of Alexandria that subscribed to Rome and Constantinople but remained largely within the boundaries of Alexandria, and the Coptic church of the majority Egyptian Christians who opposed Chalcedon and eventually became independent from Rome and Constantinople.

The Coptic church was the branch that would endure and become identified with Egyptian Christianity. During these early centuries, Egypt was considered a Christian nation, and was responsible for evangelizing other nations, especially Ethiopia and Nubia. Monasticism continued to flourish, and the Copts established their Egyptian Christian identity through the arts, including Coptic literature, paintings, textiles, and architecture. Due to its break with Rome and Constantinople, this Egyptian church gradually came to experience pressure and persecution from the Byzantine Empire. Despite the challenges, by 700 Coptic Christianity had spread throughout the entire Nile Valley.

So deeply planted was the Christian faith in Egypt that even after the Arab invasion, the rise of Islam was unable to completely uproot it. As Theodore Partrick so aptly puts it, though "Islam was to displace rather quickly the churches in the rest of North Africa...it was never able to displace the Coptic Church in Egypt."[3]

---

3 Theodore Hall Partrick, *Traditional Egyptian Christianity: A History of the Coptic Orthodox Church* (Greensboro, NC: Fisher Park Press, 1996), 44.

THE ARAB CONQUEST
AND THE RISE OF ISLAM

It had been almost two hundred years since the disagreement at Chalcedon had caused the Egyptian church to break away from the church of the Roman and Byzantine empires. In those two centuries, the Egyptian church had developed its own national identity, becoming more Coptic and less Hellenistic. Christianity had grown and flourished throughout the country despite Egypt being subject to a larger, foreign empire that its people did not particularly care for. It was probably not terribly distressing to the Egyptians when in 641 the Byzantine ruler of Egypt was conquered by an Arab general, Amr ibn al-As, and Egypt became a province of a new Islamic empire, the capital of which was Damascus and then later Baghdad.

They could not have anticipated at that time that this Arab conquest would eventually result in Islam becoming the dominant religion of Egypt, in Arabic replacing Coptic as the national language, even in the church, or in Cairo replacing Alexandria as the capital city of Egypt and becoming the new center of Islamic civilization.

The situation within this new empire began fairly well for the Egyptians. They at first considered that the Islamists had helped liberate them from the oppressive Roman emperors; initially the Copts were treated well by the Muslims as *dhimmis*, a "protected" people.[4] The prophet Muhammad was said to have had a Coptic concubine, Marya, with whom he had a son. This son died at a young age along with his mother. Upon Marya's death, Muhammad had honored her by honoring her people; he commanded that the Egyptians be protected and esteemed. General Amr took this charge to heart and was friendly with the Copts to the point of bringing back a banished patriarch named Benjamin, who had been exiled by the last Byzantine emperor, and returning him to the charge of his church.

The relations between Muslims and Christians thus began cordially, especially under the Umayyad Dynasty (661–750). According to the Quran, "There shall be no compulsion in religion" (Sura 2:256). For the first century or so under Islamic rule, the Egyptian Christians maintained relative freedom and autonomy in their religious practice and in their civil affairs, though they were not considered equal citizens with the Muslims. As

---

4 From the Arabic word meaning "protected," *dhimmis* are non-Muslim citizens living within an Islamic state, the implication being that they were protected by their Muslim rulers from foreign invaders. However, this "protection" came at a high price and functioned more as exploitation: the *dhimmis* were forced to pay crippling taxes and endure discriminating social disabilities, which often led to persecution.

second-class citizens, they were obliged to pay taxes to the Muslim government, including the *jizya* (poll tax), charged to adult, non-Muslim men, and the *kharag* (property tax), though Muslims paid neither. They were also barred from serving in the military. Despite this, Egyptian Christians, especially of the upper classes, still retained property rights and occupied important positions in business and in state government and administration, though they were usually excluded from the highest offices. The church also remained intact since Christians at this point were still the majority. Eventually, however, this favored position changed for the Copts.

Through marriage and social pressures, including the higher taxation of Christians, many Copts began converting to Islam. In addition, the Islamic caliphs (political and religious leaders) began imposing harsher restrictions upon the Egyptians. In 706, the use of the Coptic language in public documents was prohibited, and Arabic became the official national language. In 722, an edict was issued for the destruction of all Christian icons, leading to a rebellion during which many Copts were slaughtered. Taxes were periodically increased, and those who could not pay were imprisoned or subjected to a public flogging. By 770, particularly around the Nile Delta, Christians had again revolted against their Muslim rulers.

These revolts continued into the Abbasid Dynasty (750–870). In one of the more serious revolts of this period against the tax collectors, thousands of Copts were killed, or were deported to Baghdad and sold as slaves. More and more self-proclaimed Christians, because of fear of persecution or increasing social pressure, converted to Islam.

By the ninth century, the number of believers in Egypt had dwindled significantly, though many were still loyal to the faith. For those who continued to hold to the name of Christ and to their national identity as Copts, conditions grew steadily worse. Discriminatory measures and laws were imposed on them that severely restricted their "freedom" of worship. For example, they were not allowed to build new churches or places of worship (or repair old ones) without first obtaining permission from the Islamic authorities. Christians had to wear distinctive clothing that set them apart as Copts. They were forbidden from erecting crosses in public, holding public processions, or riding horses (they were permitted to ride donkeys only).

In 868, monks were no longer exempt from paying the *jizya* tax. From 1003–1013, under the Fatimid Dynasty (969–1171) such discriminatory laws became very coercive and were extended not only to Christians, but to other religious minorities as well, including Jews and even some Sunni

Muslims.[5] Under these measures, non-Muslims were prohibited from holding government office, and their personal goods and property were confiscated. Several churches and monasteries were destroyed. Rioting against Christians was encouraged, and the threat of job dismissal for being a Christian was always a looming possibility. The Christian population continued to shrink, and Coptic Christianity was slowly absorbed into the ruling Islamic state. By the end of the tenth century, Coptic authors began to write in Arabic and Christians Arabized their names. In most of Egypt, Muslims became the majority.

Nevertheless, Christianity was not dead, as God was not through with His church in Egypt. Though Arabic was the official everyday language, many Copts continued to use Coptic in private quarters, especially for worship. In the monastic communities of the desert, the Christian faith was still alive and well, despite many monasteries having been destroyed. The seventh through the twelfth centuries saw a flourishing of Coptic art

---

5 The Sunni sect of Islam was actually the majority group, while the Shiite sect (to which the Fatimids belonged) was the minority. These two sects often came into conflict because of their differing philosophies, as Sunnis were typically considered more orthodox and Shiites more liberal. The Fatimids got their name from Fatima, the daughter of the prophet Muhammad, and they recognized her husband, Ali, as the first legitimate caliph after Muhammad.

AL-AZHAR UNIVERSITY

Before the Fatimids, the ruling Arab caliphs of
Egypt resided in Baghdad, then the center of
the Islamic world. That changed in 969 when
the Fatimids took power. Caliph al-Moizz created a new capital city in Cairo and in 970 had
a new mosque built—al-Azhar—which also
functioned as a school of learning. A few years
later, unlike other caliphs before him, al-Moizz
came to reside in Cairo, and the city, including
al-Azhar mosque, soon became the new center
for Islamic civilization.

By the time of the Mamluk Dynasty, the
prominence of the al-Azhar university had
grown, and it became known as the hub of
Sunni Islam, as it is still considered today.
Though the university has undergone measures
and reforms throughout the years to national-
ize and modernize it, now, as then, the main
subjects of study include Islamic law, Islamic
theology, and the Arabic language.

in the form of weavings, painting, and architecture. Several churches were built even after the
Arab invasion. Coptic architecture, especially, was
noticed and respected by certain influential Muslims, who invited Christian architects to contribute

to their own religious or government buildings. Occasionally an Islamic ruler with more tolerance for the Copts would ascend to the throne and offer Christians a brief respite from their troubles, allowing the church to recuperate somewhat. These times were rare, but they offered Egyptian Christianity a chance to survive.

By the time of the Crusades under the Ayyubid Dynasty (1171–1250), Egyptian Christians were again expelled from government because of their supposed sympathetic ties to the Franks (or European Christians). One of the major Coptic churches in Alexandria was also demolished so the Franks would not use it as a fortress against the Islamists. Despite this, and due to national loyalty, the Egyptians ultimately joined with the Muslims in fighting against the Europeans during the fifth crusade from 1218–22.

A new Muslim dynasty, the Mamluks (1250–1517), began another wave of periodic intolerance and persecution against Christians. The Mamluks came from warrior stock, having originally been foreign slaves of the Ayyubid rulers and forced to serve as their bodyguards and soldiers. As rewards for their faithful service, many of the Mamluk soldiers had risen to high army positions and been given gifts and property of their own. They become so powerful in and of themselves that they overtook the Ayyubid sultan and named their own sultan, becoming the next ruling Arab dynasty in Egypt.

The Mamluks were ruthless rulers, perhaps because of their military background, and had little sympathy for the Copts. They had no common aspirations with the Copts, nor did they speak their language. Sultan Baybars I (1260–77) had accused Christians of setting fires to parts of Cairo and imposed impossibly high taxes upon them to raise money for a military campaign. Serious conflicts between Muslims and Copts around 1320 resulted in a large number of churches and monasteries being burned down and destroyed. The rulers of the Mamluk Dynasty tried eight times between 1279 and 1447 to expel Coptic civil servants from government posts, among other things. Many Copts were well-educated, however, and their skills as bureaucrats, craftsmen, merchants, architects, physicians, and bookkeepers were recognized as of use to the country.

Nevertheless, the Mamluks always tried to suppress Coptic influence or activity, and thus the Egyptian Christians suffered under their rule. Despite the trouble it posed to the Copts, the Mamluk Dynasty was characterized by much political instability. Mamluk sultans often inherited the throne not through family succession, but through power and dominance. Most were betrayed somehow or assassinated; they rarely died of natural causes, and because of this their reigns were mainly short-lived.

A testament to the vitality and durability of the Coptic faith lies in the Coptic cultural renaissance. Despite declining numbers of Christians in Egypt, the thirteenth century saw the Golden Age of Copto-Arabic literature. Many church texts (and some secular texts) were produced in Arabic during this time, including canon law, Coptic synaxary, Coptic grammar, expositions of Christian doctrine, biblical commentary, glossaries of church books, defenses of the faith, poetry, history, literature, and Gospel translations. Unfortunately, by the fourteenth century, Copts so decreased in number and became such a minority in their own country that Coptic recorded history came to an end. The Coptic church, though always somewhat tolerated, continued to decline in Egypt during the fourteenth through nineteenth centuries.

STORY FROM HISTORY: BULUS (PAUL) AL-HABIS

It was the year 1265, and Mamluk Sultan Baybars I had recently come into power under a new Muslim dynasty in Egypt. His people were renowned as warriors. They had been the military elite of the Ayyubid sultan, and had so distinguished themselves and risen in power that they challenged their masters and became the new rulers.

The wars against the crusading European invaders were still going strong after more than a century and a half of conflict, and Baybars I was in the center of the action. To raise money for his military campaign in Syria against the Crusaders, he imposed heavier taxes and fines upon the Egyptian Christians. Neither he nor his people had much sympathy for them. The Copts were a minority by this time, and since the beginning of the Islamists' rule they had been used to being taxed. It was the price they paid for being a "protected" people, after all. The world was composed of those who wielded power dictating and ordering life for all the rest, and those who were subject to them: those who were rulers and those who were the ruled. The Copts were useful to the Mamluks because they cultivated the land, grew the food, made the goods, and paid the taxes that supported the Mamluks. Aside from that, what else were the Copts good for, and what rights should they expect? They definitely weren't needed for helping to run the affairs of state.

The sultan figured that the Copts knew this. They had known it for several centuries by this time. Besides that, they were a nuisance of a people. Recently, several fires had been set around the capital city, Cairo, which demolished over sixty houses. Certain Christians (and Jews) had been blamed for it. Though nobody could be certain who was responsible for the fires, it seemed convenient that the Christians should be targeted. It might have been anybody, but if it had been the Christians, it would offer a legitimate excuse to raise their tribute taxes. If they refused to pay the fine for the fires, the sultan would destroy their quarters of the city and have the accused persons burned alive.

Baybars I presented this ultimatum to the Copts, but the sum of money imposed on them was too high for them to pay. A monk named Bulus al-Habis, also known as Paul, heard about the plight of the Egyptian Christians in Cairo. He had once been a scribe, having come from a respectable Coptic family of scribes, before taking his vows. He had left a promising career to become a monk. Though he had mainly lived in solitude, residing in a cave in the Red Mountain south of Cairo, he still maintained ties to society, particularly through his money. He traveled all throughout Egypt, teaching and preaching, and also offering financial assistance wherever he found need. Following the example of the great Desert Father, Anthony, who gave away all he had before becoming a monk, Paul also gave away his personal wealth, but he did so throughout his life as a monk to whomever he came into contact with, whether an individual or an entire community. He helped pay debts and taxes, and free prisoners.

When Paul came upon the plight of the Christians in Cairo, it wasn't the first time he had helped to settle an unjust government-imposed fine. Though he was but a monk and lived in a humble, meager way among others like him, he had the financial means to pay the total amount charged on the community. His source of wealth was private, but it was his to use in whatever way he chose, and he chose to give it selflessly to his fellow brothers and sisters in trouble in order to prevent further misfortune from falling upon them.

Paul paid the fine, freeing the Christians from their harsh financial obligation and at the same time inciting the curiosity and displeasure of the sultan and his Muslim clerics. They felt threatened by Paul's popularity, particularly since the monk's source of wealth was a mystery they were unable to penetrate. Why a humble Egyptian man of God should be endowed with such wealth perhaps also provoked jealousy among the Muslim nobility and priesthood. Paul was summoned to appear before the sultan in the citadel. He was offered food and drink, invited to stay, and asked about the source of his money. Because Paul refused to disclose this information, the sultan's clerics pressured the sultan to have him executed, which Baybars accordingly did. Paul was condemned to death and executed for displaying God's love in a practical, tangible way to the poor and oppressed people of Egypt. He is remembered today as a Coptic saint.

THE WEST DISCOVERS EGYPT: THE OTTOMAN EMPIRE AND FRENCH OCCUPATION

The Ottoman Turks gained control of Egypt in 1517, ending Mamluk rule, and Egypt was once again absorbed by a foreign power: the Ottoman Empire. These rulers were also Muslims, and had their capital city in Istanbul, the former site of Constantinople. As a province of the Ottoman Empire, Egypt was ruled under a *pasha*, or governor, appointed by the sultan who resided in the capital.

The Christians in Egypt fared little better under their Turkish overlords than they had under their Arab overlords. The situation may have been worse, in fact, due to its exploitive nature. The Turks just built on the Mamluk system, especially since the Mamluks still exerted significant influence as a ruling class in Egypt. Like the Mamluks, the Turks cared very little for the nation or its people, interested only in what Egypt might offer them in strengthening their empire. Almost immediately upon gaining control of the country, the Turkish sultan, Selim, transported much of Egypt's key talent—merchants, craftsmen, engineers, doctors, religious leaders, etc.—to Istanbul for the betterment of his own country, and used Egypt's resources to build up the Ottoman navy.

During the next couple of centuries, as the Roman Catholic church in Rome attempted several times to regain ties with the Alexandrian church, many Christians sought help and refuge from Rome since the Catholic church was a staunch enemy of the Turks. It wasn't difficult for Egyptian Christians to maintain contact with the Western church since Alexandria and Cairo were two of the world's most significant trade centers at the time, and they were accustomed to receiving visitors from all over, especially Europe. Though the Catholic church was never fully able to reunify with the church of Alexandria, it still managed to establish several missions and monasteries in Egypt.

The Roman Catholics weren't the only foreign group to have a presence in Egypt during the Ottoman rule in the sixteenth and seventeenth centuries. Protestant groups such as the Lutherans and the Moravian Brethren also sent missionaries to Egypt, paving the way for later Protestant missions in the country. Their influence was countered by Rome, but not completely eliminated.

Despite these Western Christian influences in Egypt, the number of Copts continued to decline under the oppression and persecution of their Islamic rulers, particularly after 1767 when the

Mamluks regained power over Egypt for a brief period of time. The political situation in Egypt deteriorated into near anarchy, and Christians were once again targeted, especially regarding financial dues to their overlords. Egypt's Coptic population, once the majority in a Christian nation, dropped to less than ten percent by the end of the eighteenth century. Egyptian Christians might have felt alone and abandoned in the world at such a low ebb in their history, but little did they know they had not been completely forgotten.

As the centuries passed and technological advances made world travel more convenient and practical, many more Westerners were coming to Egypt for purposes other than missions. Whether merchants, businessmen, traders, or tourists, Egypt saw an influx of visitors beginning in the sixteenth century, many of whom would leave with collected information and artifacts to take back to Europe. Much of this information regarded the Coptic, or native, people of Egypt, and many of these artifacts were Coptic texts including grammars and lexicons that had been purchased from monasteries. During the sixteenth through eighteenth centuries, many manuscripts about the Copts and their language were composed and shared throughout Europe. Besides literature being produced about the Copts, original texts and manuscripts from Egypt were donated to libraries and museums in Europe, such as the Vatican Library in Rome and the British Museum in London.

Soon the West changed from curious friend to conqueror. In 1798, Napoleon's forces arrived in Egypt, hoping to expand the French empire into the East. Along with thousands of soldiers, Napoleon brought with him over one hundred experts and Egyptologists to further study the country and learn how it might best be governed. The Copts might have initially hoped that their situation would improve under the French, whom they considered fellow Christians, especially since they had come under the guise of "liberating" Egypt. But Egypt's Christians were disappointed. The French were liberators only from the rule of the Turkish *pashas*, and they found it politically expedient to ally themselves with Egypt's Muslim majority.

Napoleon even proclaimed himself a Muslim to win Egypt's favor. His administrators paid little heed to the Christian minority and did little to improve the situation for the Copts, who continued to be oppressed and persecuted by the Islamic population. The same discrimination that had always occurred against the Copts and Jews continued to preside—the distinctive clothing setting them apart as second-class citizens, the disabling taxes, and the unfair restrictions on mode of travel (Copts still could not ride horses, only donkeys).

Napoleon Bonaparte

French rule was short-lived, lasting only three years, however, and by 1801 the last of Napoleon's forces had left Egypt. Centuries of military competition between France and England came into effect as the British swooped in to aid the Ottomans in regaining control of Egypt. It was strategic on the part of the British: they didn't want the French blocking their trade routes to India. The Turks then once again held Egypt as a province under the Ottoman Empire, and there followed continued Christian persecution. Many Copts had served in the French military alongside Napoleon and had supported his campaign against Egypt's Ottoman rulers. Because of this, many of them were accused of cooperating with the French and were killed.

After centuries of power shifts and intermittent persecution, the Egyptian Christians were soon to find a brief reprieve under one of Egypt's most famous figures: Muhammad Ali.

THE WEST DISCOVERS EGYPT: THE NINETEENTH CENTURY AND BRITISH OCCUPATION

With the departure of the French from Egypt, the Turkish sultan reclaimed his role as the head of Egypt. The French occupation had done nothing to improve the tense relations between Muslims and Christians, nor had the French altered the unjust treatment of the Egyptian Christians by the Islamic population. The French had wasted no time in allying themselves with the Muslim majority, recognizing Egypt as an Arab, Islamic state. Those who still claimed their ancient Coptic roots, and especially those who claimed the name of Christ, were overlooked and marginalized as they had been for over a thousand years.

Though Egypt was under the dominion of the Ottoman Empire, the real power behind the nation was the Mamluk ruling class as before. But the resurgence of the Mamluk regime in Egypt was short-lived due to a man named Muhammad Ali, an officer in the Ottoman army. Muhammad Ali rose to power in 1805 (but not completely overthrowing the Mamluks until 1811) and later proclaimed himself the *khedive*, or ruler, of Egypt, a post he held until his death in

1848. Ali believed that all people should be considered equal regardless of religion or nationality. He felt strongly that it was time for Egypt to be brought into the modern era through reforms in administration, education, agricultural production, and industrialization. He also aimed to establish a national Egyptian army.

Recognizing the Copts' Western ties, Ali believed it advantageous to support the oppressed minority. Thus, Egyptian Christians (as well as other minorities) enjoyed a temporary respite under Ali and his successors throughout the nineteenth century. For the first time in a long time, the Copts and the Christian faith were able to thrive. Ali helped restore order to the monasteries, which by that time had decreased to only seven. Whereas previous rulers had scoffed at the idea that the Copts should take part in leading the country, Muhammad Ali allowed them to come into government circles once more. He employed many Armenian Christians in his government and even had a Christian as his close financial advisor for many years. Copts were able to freely practice and cultivate their professions, raise their social status, and once more own land through opportunities for private investment. Another momentous change occurred for the Copts when during the reign of Muhammad Said (1854–63) the *jizya* poll tax was finally abolished and the Copts were permitted to serve in the military for the first time since the Arab conquest. Finally, after years of living as second-class citizens in their own country, the Copts achieved full Egyptian citizenship under Muhammad Tewfiq (1879–92).

During this era the educational situation for Egyptian Christians improved as well. Muhammad Ali had opened state, or civil, schools that were most likely open to all, regardless of religion. And more foreign missionaries were arriving in Egypt, such as those with the Church Missionary Society of the Church of England, who established schools for the education of church leaders. But the real educational reformer of the mid nineteenth century was Cyril IV, who was the Coptic patriarch from 1854 to 1861. Known as "The Reformer," Cyril was almost wholly responsible for improving the educational system for the Copts. He established a Coptic Patriarchal College, as well as a boys' school and two girls' schools. He, like the English Anglican missionaries, was concerned with educating church leaders and would meet regularly with the clergy. He also founded printing presses and developed relationships with other Christian communities in Egypt, including the Greek and Anglican communities.

During the rulership of the *khedives*, as they attempted to modernize Egypt based on a Western model, Egypt functioned for the most part free from Western interference. But Britain gradually intervened first to guide and then to control the political affairs of Egypt. Khedive Ismail was forced out of office, and Muhammad Tewfiq was installed by the British. By 1882, Britain had colonial control of Egypt, which they maintained through WWII.

Like the French, the British associated their rule with the dominant Muslim population. Lord Cromer took charge during the early years of the British occupation. Though his goals and reforms focused on leading Egypt into political and financial stability, including organizational and technical improvements, he believed that Islamic customs should be honored and preserved. He made the Quran the only officially recognized religious book in Egypt. Likewise, he decreed that the Muslim sheikh be the only religious teacher allowed in government schools. He also lowered the investment in education.

Once again, the Christians in Egypt were disillusioned with the British as they had been with the French: the supposedly Christian nation of Britain seemed to have an agenda of promoting Islam instead of sympathizing with and aiding the Copts in their trials.

COURAGEOUS WORDS
FROM EGYPTIAN CHRISTIANS

*"Jesus Christ is worth doing this for.
We have to. It is the gift of suffering for Him.
And I believe our country will change
as a direct result."*

—MARY, a Muslim-background believer
who ministers to young women who have
converted from Islam to Christianity

*"We ought to obey God rather than men, for
our loyalty to Him surpasses all other loyalties... We prefer to die upright than to live
stained. As Christians we will serve you.
But we will not relinquish our faith in our
Lord, and this we openly declare."*

—MEN OF THE THEBAN LEGION in the early fourth
century, decimated for their allegiance to Christ
(To read more about the Theban Legion, see page 30.)

*"Jesus never promised that we would have a
rose-filled world. As I go along with Christ, I
share His suffering and I know the trouble
that I face is because I walk with Him. Jesus*

is worth it, you know. I love Him so much. The secret of joy is having a real bond with Christ. We can't help but be happy. In the fiery furnace, Shadrach, Meshach, and Abednego said, 'Even if we are not saved from the fire, we will believe.'

—NOORA, a Muslim-background believer who was brutally beaten by her husband for her Christian faith

"The Lord Christ I confess, on Him I rely, in His name I die, and through Him I live forever."

—DEMIANA, martyred in the early fourth century *(To read more about Demiana, see page 33.)*

"I'll never leave the Lord. I love Him. I ... will remain a Christian and will die a Christian."

—HANI, a Coptic Christian killed for his faith

"I don't know what will happen next. I only know that I love Christ and live for him, whatever troubles I may face."

—FATMA, a Muslim-background believer whose family threatened to kill her if she didn't marry a Muslim man

EGYPT

"Jesus said in the world you will be persecuted. 'You will have persecution, but make sure that you trust Me because I have overcome the world.' When I read this verse I thought we are too far from heaven because this didn't happen to me. And when this day came, this trial, I felt heaven is near for us."

—MEGAD, an Egyptian Christian whose village was attacked by a mob of Muslim men

EGYPT FOR
THE EGYPTIANS

By the early 1900s, a strong sense of nationalism had emerged in opposition to British rule. The Copts were at the forefront of some of the nationalist movements that arose, especially those that claimed true Egypt as everything that came before the Arab conquest and the spread of Islam. Coinciding with this, and possibly a motivating force for it, was a burgeoning interest in "Egyptology" beginning in the late 1800s. Archeologists from all over Europe, including England, France, and Austria, came to Egypt in search of ancient sites and artifacts. Though this interest mainly revolved around Egypt's pharaohs, Coptic heritage, especially in the form of textiles and architecture, was also a subject of many excavations, particularly as museums wished to add to their collections. More and more research about pre-Islamic Egypt was conducted, and just like in the eighteenth century, books were published in Europe concerning the Coptic people, their history, and their language.

Though all of this archeological study and literary research came from outside Egypt, from within the country, a sense of reclaiming "Egypt for the Egyptians" arose and permeated many

EGYPT

nationalist movements. The Egyptian Christians in particular grew bold and demanded certain rights and recognition that had been denied them for generations. They took part in demonstrations and revolts. Despite these movements, the British occupation persisted and its rulers began appointing national kings for Egypt. During WWI, an heir of Muhammad Ali was set upon the Egyptian throne as ruler. In 1917, the British installed Fuad I as sultan, and later as king.

About this same time, around 1910, the Coptic community was experiencing another sort of movement, though not a political one. A deacon of the church, Habib Guirguis, was almost solely responsible for establishing Sunday schools within the Coptic church. Modeled after Protestant Sunday schools, they were hugely successful and so popular that before long every Coptic church in Egypt had adopted them. In 1918, Guirguis had established a formal committee of Sunday schools, which was responsible not only for developing the curriculum, but for opening new schools in other cities and villages. These schools were characterized by classes for every grade, youth meetings, teacher meetings, and prayer groups. This is what so distinguished them, and why Sunday schools were so revolutionary in the Coptic community: while other educational efforts in the church focused on the education of the clergy only, Sunday schools offered guidance, encouragement, and instruction to everyone in the church.

In the 1930s, other groups and movements arose that associated nationalism with a militant Islamic agenda. One of these groups was the Muslim Brotherhood, Egypt's oldest and largest Islamic organization. Whereas in earlier nationalist movements, Christians would often join with Muslims in the fight for "Egypt for the Egyptians," the Muslim Brotherhood's agenda of Islamic supremacy was so far removed from the Copts' desire that the attitude of national unity among Christians and Muslims was soon lost.

The Muslim Brotherhood was established in 1928 by Hassan al-Banna, in the city of Ismailiya, in response to the Salafist movement. The word *salaf* in Arabic refers to the prophet Mohammed's companions and early followers. The Salafists believed in a return to the principles and traditions of the earliest form of Islam, feeling that the deterioration of the Ottoman Empire and the

Mohammed Badie, 8th General Leader of the Muslim Brotherhood

modernization of Egypt, including the acceptance of civic over religious education, would result in subjugation of Muslims by Western "infidels." They began proselytizing and encouraging young Egyptians to embrace traditional Islam. The Muslim Brotherhood grew out of this movement. Because it sought the removal of British colonial control (and all other Western influences), the Brotherhood soon grew into a highly political movement for the spread of Islam and the creation of a religious state governed by Sharia law. In 1935, the Brotherhood held an Organizing Congress in which they stated that their program was the embodiment of Islam, adopted a number of resolutions that sought obedience and unity from all members, and declared that any deviation from the program would be considered an offense to the Islamic religion. This brought them into conflict with liberal Islamists who believed in equal citizenship and rights among Muslims, Christians, and Jews living in a secular state. The writings of Brotherhood member Sayyid Qutb would later inspire the formation of other radical Islamic groups such as Islamic Jihad and al-Qaida.

During the 1952 Egyptian revolution, Egypt's British-installed monarchy finally collapsed in what is widely called a military coup led by Colonel Gamal Abdel Nasser. Theodore Partrick has said that "1952 marked a return to despotism,"

President Nasser

and that "Nasser's brand of nationalism risked leaving the Copts out in its 'return to Islam.'"[6] Egypt became a republic, and Nasser appointed himself its first president. Nasser wanted modernization, reform, and socialization of Egypt. As a secularist, he ultimately desired a non-religious Arab state. In 1956, a new constitution drawn up under Nasser's presidency called Egypt an Arab nation and included Socialist principles.

Though Nasser's Arabization of Egypt was meant to be secular and liberal rather than religious, it ultimately sparked the beginnings of the Islamization of society. As Egyptian writer and historian Tarek Osman put it in his book *Egypt on the Brink*, "Immersing Egypt, politically and culturally, in the Arab world...entailed a thorough redirection of society towards the Islamic culture that had ruled the Arabs' historical heartland for fourteen centuries."[7]

---

6 Theodore Hall Partrick, *Traditional Egyptian Christianity: A History of the Coptic Orthodox Church* (Greensboro, NC: Fisher Park Press, 1996), 155.

7 Tarek Osman, *Egypt on the Brink: From Nasser to Mubarak* (London: Yale University Press, 2011), 152.

Inevitably, during Nasser's regime, the economic and political power of the Copts eroded. The influence of notable Coptic citizens in the affairs of state declined dramatically. Under new agrarian reforms limiting the amount of acreage individuals could own, many Copts lost a significant portion of their land holdings, and consequently much of their wealth and income. Many Egyptian Christians emigrated in the 1960s to America, England, Australia, and Canada in order to flee discrimination and persecution. Those who stayed in Egypt drew closer to the church to preserve their Christian identity and heritage, and to find solace and direction. Many young middle-class Egyptian Christians left their academic or business careers to become priests in a kind of "revival" of the church.

Upon his death in 1970, Nasser was succeeded as president by Anwar Sadat. Sadat was more tolerant of Christians and spearheaded a peace accord in 1978 with Israel. But he was unpopular with Islamic fundamentalists.

The 1970s brought troubles for Egyptian Christians from organizations such as the Islamic Group and the Muslim Brotherhood. Muslims were alarmed and threatened by the revival of the Coptic language and by Christian groups that had been busy evangelizing, building churches, developing schools, and providing social services to Christian families including the poor, unemployed, elderly, students, and young graduates. The role of Sunday schools had also grown, becoming key places for Christian social activity. Clusters of Christians emerged in the form of Christian-based companies that hired mainly believers and universities with predominantly Christian professors. In addition, Christian communities had developed a greater awareness of their importance in participation in the military and politics, and thus many Christians were involved in sociopolitical organizations. The Coptic church especially was seen by the government as a political entity itself, striving to undermine the Muslim majority's attempts to institute Sharia into Egyptian law.

Based on all these perceived threats by Christians, societies of university students began organized attacks on believers. Churches were bombed, and Christian leaders, whether bishops or businessmen, were attacked and sometimes assassinated.

Sadat had little control over the ensuing chaos, and was perhaps seen as favoring one side over the other. The government's cooperation with the Coptic

President Sadat

church then deteriorated in an attempt to retain national unity. Sadat came to believe that the Coptic leadership was planning to secede from the Egyptian state and establish its own capital city. He did not wish the government to be undermined in such a way, and therefore had Coptic Pope Shenouda III removed from office and exiled. Over one hundred Coptic bishops, priests, and other religious leaders were also arrested and imprisoned. Several Muslim organizations were banned as well. Then, in 1981, Sadat was assassinated by militant Muslims and Hosni Mubarak was installed as president.

Mubarak worked to suppress Islamic radicals, though he couldn't completely eradicate persecution and discrimination against Christians, who were being increasingly marginalized by the majority population. Challenges they faced included limited employment opportunities (job openings for Muslims only), segregated university classrooms, and the failure of Christian politicians to win elections in Muslim-majority constituencies. Believing that Egypt's identity had moved from a liberal and tolerant nationalism to Islamic religiosity, with Islam becoming firmly embedded in politics and in societal attitudes, behaviors, and speech, Christians had gradually been forced to withdraw from greater society to find refuge. Many found this refuge in economic and social enclaves. Predominantly Christian neighborhoods began to emerge. In the 1980s and 1990s, there was an upsurge in church building, particularly in areas where the Muslim Brotherhood had a strong influence. Christian media in the form of satellite channels and Internet sites, as well as an official publication of the Egyptian church, also gained prominence. Despite all this, many Christians made a literal retreat in the 1990s and 2000s by emigrating like they had in the 1960s.

President Mubarak worked somewhat to remedy the situation for Christians. In January 1985 he reinstated Pope Shenouda III. He appointed Christian politicians to the parliament, and placed some Christian officers in marginal positions in the interior ministries of environment and emigration. He made Easter and Christmas (January 7) national holidays. He viewed political and militant Islamism as "un-Egyptian," and disagreed with the Muslim Brotherhood's creation of religion-based political parties. Though Mubarak seemed to favor and even endorse Christianity, he was criticized for using Egyptian Christians to serve his

Source: Presidenza della Repubblica

President Mubarak

own purposes in his struggle with political Islam. His "support" of Christians was largely strategic and self-serving. In the same way, he used factions of the Islamic movement to discredit political and militant Islam, particularly the Muslim Brotherhood, especially in 1980s and 1990s.

Militant Islamists had a twofold purpose: they wished to challenge (or overthrow) the government regime to bend it toward their ideology; and they desired to purge Egypt of all infidels (non-Muslims). Ultimately they wanted the Islamization of society. They saw the current government as waging a "war against Islam."

Despite Mubarak's attempts to suppress and contain militant Islamism, it continued to spread. With it, greater violence and dissatisfaction with the Mubarak regime increased as well. Though the majority of Egyptians supported Mubarak's efforts to combat the militants and opposed the use of violence to pursue religious ends, political Islam managed to gain popularity through the years. Its beliefs and ideology bled into civilian Egypt, particularly in the 2000s, so that many Egyptians came to view their president and their governmental regime as unsympathetic toward the ordinary people's feelings and desires. Demonstrations, riots, and strikes followed in which Egyptians voiced their opposition to the Mubarak regime. The years 2005 to 2009 were especially wrought with violent demonstrations and riots against the president. Most people were particularly unhappy with the government's foreign policy doctrine—as a supposed US ally and "friend of Israel"—and disapproved of Egypt's support of Israel's war against Hamas rule from December 2008 to January 2009. They ultimately believed the Egypt Mubarak represented was his own vision and not that of the ordinary people. In addition to the country's deteriorating economy, citizens were angry about the government's use of coercion and its interference in civil affairs and organizations such as the universities.

This discontent continued until it escalated into the 2011 Revolution, when Mubarak was forced to resign due to harsh and violent protests against his presidency.

MUSLIM-BACKGROUND BELIEVERS

It would be inaccurate to say that the Coptic people, who trace their roots back to pre-Islamic Egypt, are the only true Egyptians, or that Copts are the only Christians in Egypt. For much of its history, Egypt has been a melting pot of cultures and civilizations, including native Egyptians, Greeks, Romans, Jews, Arabs, and Armenians, among others. For thousands of years, Egypt has possessed an undeniable charm and fascination drawing many to visit or settle there. The Nile River Valley is one of the most fertile agricultural areas in the world. Alexandria and Cairo have always been significant historical, educational, and cultural world centers. Egypt's location, especially in the pre-modern world, has always been convenient and strategic for trade as well as travel. Many have come and gone from Egypt; many have come and stayed.

For thousands of years Egypt had been ruled by foreigners, from the time of Alexander the Great in 332 BC to the British-installed *khedives* of the first half the twentieth century. From Greeks and Romans to the Arab Muslims, from the North African Fatimids to the Kurd Ayyubids, from the Mamluks of Turkish and Caucasian descent to

the Albanian and Anatolian Mohammad Ali dynasty, Egypt had never seen a native Egyptian ruler
before the mid-twentieth century when Nasser
came along. Each of these groups contributed
cultural elements—including language, religious
observation, food, and dress—that were either
forced upon the Egyptians or were ultimately absorbed into their pre-existing structures. Over
time, these new elements of culture became so
intermingled and widely practiced that they became identified with the nation's roots. Thus Egypt
has seen a massive transformation over the centuries regarding what constitutes "Egyptianism,"
and what makes a true Egyptian.

For not all Egyptians, and not all Christians,
are Copts. Though the Copts are the largest Christian minority group in the entire Middle East,
their numbers have diminished so severely that
they represent a small percentage of the Egyptian
population. Today many Egyptians are, in fact, of
Arab descent and Muslim. Though Copts have
historically been persecuted based on their eth-
nicity as well as their religion, Muslims who convert
to Christianity are persecuted solely for bearing
the name of Christ and for their Christian witness.

Muslims in Egypt are taught that Islam is the
"true religion," that the Holy Books of Scripture
(the Bible) have been corrupted, and that the
Quran is the only pure revelation of God. They

are told that all Christians and other nonbelievers are infidels, and are highly discouraged from associating with them. But there are many young Muslims who find themselves feeling dissatisfied or confused with their religion, and they ask questions and seek answers. Many who try to ask their families or their local sheiks about Jesus or Christianity are quickly reprimanded and their questions dismissed. Muslim seekers will often track down Bibles and study the Word on their own, risking a scolding or a beating if the Bible is discovered. If Muslims do convert to Christianity, they are considered traitors and infidels, and are typically pressured by their families to return to Islam. The means can range from silent treatment to physical separation or isolation from the family, to threats and beatings, to imprisonments or institutionalizations in compliance with state security forces.

Many Muslims who have converted to Christianity are ultimately disowned by their families and thrown out of their houses to fend for themselves. They lose family, friends, and sometimes their jobs or even their lives. Though the law in Egypt loosely allows freedom of religion, including freedom to convert from one religion to another, Muslims who convert to Christianity are legally forbidden from changing their religion or their names on their official ID cards. Because they still carry Muslim names, police forces will turn them away from entering churches. Women with Muslim names are not permitted to marry Christian men and are instead pressured or forced to marry Muslims. The children of women designated as Muslims (even if they are Christians) are considered Muslim as well and educated as such. The law in Egypt caters to Islam in its claim of freedom of conversion.

For the sake of his children, Mohammed Hegazy filed a lawsuit against the government in August 2007 to be allowed to change the religious designation on his ID card from Muslim to Christian—the first Christian to do such a thing in Egypt. He wasn't worried about himself at all. A former Muslim who had met his Savior Jesus, Hegazy had already come out publicly with his Christian faith and suffered harassment for it. He was imprisoned several times by state security authorities and tortured to renounce his newfound beliefs. Held in prison, Hegazy was hung upside down by his feet and beaten severely. He was given electrical shocks all over his body.

Hegazy also received several *fatwas*, which are official Islamic death threats sanctioned by local Muslim sheiks. With these against him, Hegazy and his family—a wife and two small children—went into hiding where they have remained.

Hegazy's lawsuit was suspended, and he was denied his request. Though he took a huge risk in fighting a legal battle for the right to officially change his religion, his main concern was for his children. Without the legal designation of "Christian" on his ID card, his children were considered Muslims and were required to be educated in an Islamic institution. Hegazy stated in a 2010 interview, "When my wife was pregnant with our first child, I had in my heart that I don't want my child to suffer like all the children of converts in Egypt. You know, the children of converts are having a dual identity—they have to be Christian at home, Muslims at school...This is really complicated for the psychology of a child to understand or to bear."

Hegazy hopes for a freer Egypt in which his children won't experience the same harassment and persecution that he has suffered, and where they can go to school without fearing for their safety. "If you don't have the right or freedom to choose your own belief," Hegazy says, "what rights do you have? What freedom do you have? I'm not afraid because I believe in Christ."

Despite such hardships faced by Muslim-background believers, these Christians have a strong desire to spread the gospel of Jesus Christ with other Muslims and to share the truth of God's love and peace that they have discovered. They wish to see their families and friends break free from their chains of hatred and discrimination under Islam. They also desire to encourage other Christians to remain strong in their faith, and they risk much to do it.

STORY OF PERSECUTION:
ABRAHAM,
A MUSLIM-BACKGROUND BELIEVER

Abraham came from a simple peasant family in Egypt, but despite their humble dwelling containing a reed carpet and an oil lamp instead of electricity for light, Abraham was happy. He attended the village Islamic school, or *kottab*, where he learned the basic subjects of reading, writing, and reciting the Quran. He studied his lessons next to a little stream outside and early on developed a reverence for God. By the time he was in middle school he grew increasingly interested in deeper forms of study and worship, so he joined the village's Sufi group regularly at the mosque for mystical worship sessions in which he would praise the prophet Muhammad.

His dedication, his thirst for learning, and his developing skills in public speaking quickly distinguished him. Still at an early age, Abraham was asked by two Muslim men one day after prayers if he would meet some of their friends and join them in a group assembly. Abraham was impressed by these men, being from the town's elite, and he commended their unity and friendliness.

Abraham began attending regular monthly meetings at the mosque with these men and their friends where they would eat together or fast and pray. They observed all the other rites of the prophet Muhammad in the strictest fashion, in their manner of walking, talking, praying, eating, drinking, and dressing. They would regularly visit other mosques, proclaiming the "Islamic Call." By fourteen years of age, Abraham was even preaching at the mosque, his first message being about the ideal way to celebrate the prophet's birthday.

The group in which Abraham had entrenched himself was a Sunni fundamentalist group, the Muslim Brethren (or Muslim Brotherhood). When Abraham's father discovered he was a part of the Muslim Brotherhood, he grew angry and warned his son about the group, encouraging him to leave it. By that time Abraham's group had an in-

A mosque in Cairo

formant who would tape their speeches, follow their movements, and report their doings to the State Security Investigations (SSI) office. Abraham's father was worried that the SSI had his son's name. He presented himself in front of the Muslim Brotherhood at the mosque one day and screamed at them to leave his son alone. He then went home and threatened Abraham, hitting him and breaking his teeth. Knowing the militant ways of the Brotherhood, he ultimately feared that Abraham would be hurt, and used all sorts of means to keep Abraham from returning to them: he burned all his religious books and even threatened to divorce his wife if Abraham ever went back.

Abraham begged his father to be allowed to just sit outside the mosque and listen to the sermons of the Brotherhood sheiks without going in. His father reluctantly agreed, but decided to accompany him. At school Abraham continued to spread the Islamic Call, delivering an Islamic public speech every morning. He grew very meticulous in his religious observance to the point of bullying his sister into wearing a veil, and forgoing shaking hands with women or listening to songs.

One day Abraham had a thought that he might win Christians to Islam. He began speaking with Christians in his school and his neighborhood, attempting to convince them that Islam was the true religion, and he read more closely what the Quran had to say about Christians. In this way he grew interested in comparing Christianity and Islam to discover what was real and what was false. He began reading Christian books, and for at least two years he studied, questioned, and struggled within himself to find answers. He felt that from what he was learning and observing, Christians were not infidels or polytheists as he had always been taught. He wondered at the disparity between the figures of Muhammad and Jesus Christ —noticing that Jesus had such an elevated status among all the prophets that history centered on Him, and that it was He who would return at the end of days as judge instead of Muhammad. According to the Quran itself, Muhammad was a man like any other who had sinned and needed to ask forgiveness, but Jesus Christ had never sinned and had no need to seek God's forgiveness. How could Christianity be inferior to Islam when Jesus Christ seemed so superior to Muhammad?

Thoughts and questions like these made Abraham restless and kept him awake at night. Even after he got rid of all of his Christian books and resolved to stop his search and focus merely on being an obedient Muslim, Abraham was still dissatisfied and felt prodded within his heart to continue seeking answers. His search came to a finale one day as he knelt in prayer, asking God to show him the truth and dedicating his life to following and serving God. Abraham repeated this prayer until he had a vision or dream of Christ coming to him and saying, "I love you." He meditated on the love of God shown to him through Jesus' sacrificial death on the cross, and suddenly Abraham knew and believed in the truth of Christ.

Abraham suddenly felt light on his feet and happy. He praised God, knowing the Lord had shown him the Way, the Truth, and the Life. A few weeks later Abraham was baptized in a private Christian home. Through all of his experience in seeking and searching, Abraham had kept a diary. One day his diary was stolen by a Muslim friend and given to the Muslim Brotherhood that Abraham had been a part of. The Brotherhood photocopied his diary and handed it out all over the village to proclaim to all that Abraham had forsaken Islam and become a Christian. Abraham was publicly shamed, along with his family. People would point fingers whenever they walked by. Abraham's friends all abandoned him, fearing that their reputations would be ruined if they were to be seen with him.

Abraham's mother would not go out in public out of humiliation at her son's conversion. One time she hit Abraham on the head with a shoe; another time, she wore black and told everyone it was because her son was dead to her and she was mourning his death. She would pray every morning to Allah to bring her son back to Islam, and once even visited a sorcerer in hopes that he would cast a spell on Abraham that would change him. Abraham prayed to the Lord during this time, and the sorcerer, unable to do anything to affect him, told Abraham's mother, "Your son is following a path that he will never leave!"

Eventually the people of the village converged on Abraham and began beating him, kicking and slapping him in front of his family to try to convert him back to Islam. When his mother attempted to intervene, they yelled at her and accused the whole family of disgracing the village. At another time the villagers surrounded Abraham's house and tried to set fire to it. The police may have intervened, but the attackers succeeded in burning some of Abraham's Christian books. Faced with threats and beatings from both his family and the public, Abraham found himself willingly spending the night in the police station many times for his safety. However, the police weren't always sympathetic or helpful to Abraham. They went into his home and confiscated his Christian materials that had not been destroyed by the villagers, and kept a twenty-four-hour watch on his house to prevent any new materials from reaching him. More than just a personal matter, it was as if the entire community was involved in trying to dissuade Abraham from his newfound faith!

But God's Word prevails even in the midst of such attempts to stamp it out. One day the newspaper arrived with an article on the front page from the Coptic Pope Shenouda. Many Bible verses were included in the article, including Genesis 26:24 and Deuteronomy 31:8, in which the Lord encourages His people not to be afraid because He is with them always. This lifted Abraham's spirits and strengthened his faith. Immediately after he received the paper, a police officer knocked on his door. One of Abraham's family members grabbed the paper from his hand and burned it. This saddened Abraham, but the very next day as he was walking around, he found a copy of the same page lying on the ground outside! To him it was a miracle, a sign of the Lord's unending, watchful presence in his life.

Abraham has experienced many miraculous signs such as this, and he is convinced without a doubt that the Lord is always with him and will never forsake him. Despite his troubles, this truth gives him a peace, courage, and resilience that his former life could never offer.

REVOLUTION
TAKES HOLD

Tensions between Christians and Muslims in Egypt reached new heights in recent years beginning with Mubarak's overthrow in 2011 and continuing to the present day. Following several days of mass protests, Hosni Mubarak was forced to resign his presidency in February 2011, but it would be almost a year and a half before Egypt saw its next president. In June 2012, Mohamed Morsi became Egypt's first democratically elected president. However, his presidency didn't last long, and it ended in much the same way as Mubarak's did. On July 3, 2013, after only a year, Morsi was deposed by the Egyptian military. Ultimately, his authoritarianism and his failure to produce positive, effective reforms for social justice and the struggling economy caused many Egyptians to be unhappy with him.

An Islamist, Morsi was a member of the Muslim Brotherhood and supported its extremist agenda, which he was accused of attempting to push into law. Under his presidency, Islamic radicals were more open in their harassment and incitement against Christians. Though Christians were not necessarily a favored minority even under Mubarak's presidency, he showed them greater tolerance and recognized when crimes were committed against them, taking steps to suppress the criminals. As a Coptic Christian, Sami, told American university professor and writer David Pinault in September 2012, "Things had been less worse for us under Mubarak." During 2011–2012 alone, after Mubarak's resignation, thousands of Egyptian Christians fled the country seeking refuge.

Another cause for opposition to Morsi's regime was his connection to a jailbreak during the 2011 revolution, in which he and eighteen other members of the Muslim Brotherhood escaped from prison, destroying records and killing police officers and prisoners in the process. Viewing him as a corrupt and unfair ruler, the Egyptian people finally rose up against him. They wanted him out.

Morsi was given an ultimatum by the Egyptian military to meet certain demands of the people or be forced out. He failed to comply with this ultimatum and was consequently arrested on July 3 and taken to jail to face various criminal charges, along with many of his allies. An interim civilian government was set up to lead the country. Those who supported Morsi's ouster considered it a continuation of the 2011 Revolution, which they believe never really ended.

Though it was the "people's will" to "liberate Egypt" that ended Morsi's presidency, Christians have borne the brunt of harassment from this event. Immediately following the president's arrest, Morsi supporters, mainly Islamists and members of the Muslim Brotherhood and the Freedom and Justice Party (a political affiliation of the Brotherhood), staged mass protests in Cairo against the action. When the military stepped in to monitor the situation, the tensions escalated. Hundreds of people were killed and thousands injured in the ensuing violence and rioting.

Ultimately, Christians were targeted by certain Muslims in retaliation for their alleged support of Morsi's removal. There followed, in mid-August 2013, a series of coordinated attacks on Christians in various parts of Egypt. Not only were Coptic, Catholic, and Protestant churches destroyed, but the homes, personal property, schools, Christian bookstores, and businesses belonging to Christians were also attacked. Open Doors reported as of August 22, 2013, that 73 churches had been destroyed, 212 Christian properties attacked, and 7 Christians killed. A news broadcast on persecution.TV of The Voice of the Martyrs (VOM) Canada called it the "worst organized violence against Christians in seven hundred years." Members of the radical Muslim Brotherhood were accused of the attacks, but nothing was verified, and they denied any involvement.

The violence against Egyptian Christians was so rampant during this time that it prompted a statement by Bishop Angaelos, an Egyptian and head of the Coptic Orthodox Church in the UK. He said in a CNN news report from August 2013, "In the past two and a half years, we've had more deaths of people just because they are Christians than in the last 20 years."

Termed the Arab Spring, this period of anti-government mass protests and uprisings that began with the 2011 Revolution still continues today. Characterized by increased violence and terrorist attacks within the country, the Arab Spring has affected countless civilians in Egypt, especially Christians.

The city of Minya, which has a large Christian population, has been one of the targets. One day in mid-August 2013, after the military broke up protest camps in Cairo, mobs converged on Minya, throwing torches and scattering its civilians. When the violence died down, several churches had been burned to the ground, along with monasteries, a Christian orphanage, a Jesuit center that worked with disabled people, schools, and Christian-owned shops. A message had been left for the people via a song that rang out from an untouched snack shop's speakers: Egypt is Islamic.

In Minya, as well as in other parts of Egypt during these attacks, police responded to calls about the church attacks only when it was too late. Some responded during the attacks, stayed only a short while, and then left, giving opportunities for the attackers to return. One of the churches destroyed in Minya was the Anba Mousa el Aswad Coptic Orthodox Church, which had undergone renovations to its sanctuary just two years before, paid for by church members' donations.

Two members of the church, Said Botros Attallah and his wife, Sahar Atteya Saadallah, received an anonymous threat days after the attack. They had just experienced the loss of their church building and were now being personally targeted. The threat insisted that the couple pay 500 Egyptian pounds, or their house would be burned down with them inside. Though threats are not new to the family, they still cause fear. "We don't sleep at all at night because we're constantly afraid they're going to come and attack. So we're listening at the window or the door all night." Despite personal threats, financial loss, the destruction of their church building, and the damage endured by their city, Attallah and Saadallah remain steadfast in their faith. "Protection is only from God," Saadallah proclaims.

Some Christians choose to remain in their homes and cities after attacks, while others have little choice but to flee. In the same Arab Spring violence that targeted the city of Minya, Christians residing in a village in Minya province called Delja were also affected. It began with Islamists issuing threats over the local mosque loudspeakers, calling on residents to take revenge on "infidel Christians" in response to the political upheaval of July 3. Samir Lamei Sakr, a human rights lawyer and a Christian, owned one of two Christian homes on the block nearest the mosque. Mobs immediately attacked both homes, the other of which belonged to his cousin. Sakr's cousin was killed and his body dragged through the street behind a vehicle. Though Sakr and his family (along with his cousin's family and other extended family members) managed to escape, his house was burned down. After that day, the city became controlled by extremist Muslims, and all Coptic Christians were threatened to leave the area. Those who stayed were targeted, threatened with loss of life or property, including theft of their land and livestock. Many were forced to pay protection money to stop the violence against them. When authorities attempted to step in to control the situation in Delja, armed men fired on them.

Samir Sakr and his family left everything behind to flee to Cairo, and they know they cannot return. "Every boy, girl, mother and father is living in terror," Sakr told a reporter in September 2013. "And not only the Christians are living in fear, but the moderate Muslims are also. Terrorism and thuggery are the only laws now."

EGYPT'S HUMAN
TRAFFICKING NETWORK

Mary Kaiser, a Christian university student studying pharmacology, went out one night with a fellow student, a Muslim girl she had befriended at school. Like many young people do, they went out for pizza and a movie. It was an ordinary night like any other until Mary began feeling ill. She seemed to be coming down with something, or perhaps it was something she ate. A taxi was ordered for her, and the last her friends saw of her that night was Mary entering the taxi to take her home. Unfortunately, Mary never arrived home that night.

Her family promptly reported her missing, and within a day the authorities had news for them. According to the police, they'd found Mary in a town outside of Cairo called Kerdasa. She had apparently converted to Islam and married a Muslim vendor. It was so swift and sudden that Mary's parents couldn't believe it. Soon afterward, Mary's parents waited at the police station to see her. Four women wearing veils over their faces arrived accompanied by four bearded men and two policemen with machine guns. As they walked past the Kaisers, Mary's father called out her name. When Mary turned around, one of the bearded men pushed her and hit her in the face. Her father screamed at them to let him speak with his daughter, but the police silenced him, told him the case was closed because Mary was now a Muslim, and sent them away.

Knowing their daughter—a devoted Christian and a shy, responsible girl who had always been very close to her family—the Kaisers believed Mary had been drugged by her Muslim friend and, like many other young Christian girls in Egypt, kidnapped in order to be forced away from her faith.

Current tactics of Muslim extremists in Egypt include abducting Christian girls, then forcing them to convert to Islam, and/or to marry Muslim men. This human trafficking network targeting Christian women has been occurring for years, and the numbers have been on the rise, especially since the January 2011 Revolution. It has expanded to include underage girls and mothers of young children. Those involved, which may include government and police authorities in cooperation with Wahhabi and Salafist Muslims, assert that the Christian women are simply leaving their families of their own free will because of love and romance. The families of the abducted women, however, know better, especially since the kidnapped women are essentially held as captives, having been torn away from their previous lives and forbidden to ever see their families again.

Two Coptic girls, fourteen-year-old Nancy Magdy Fathy and her sixteen-year-old cousin Christine Ezzat Fathy, disappeared on their way to church on June 12, 2011. To demand their return, Coptic supporters of the missing girls staged a two-day sit-in before the Minya Security Headquarters building. Rumors and reports began circulating in the media, bringing attention to the case. The girls' parents believed two Muslim brothers from a neighboring village had kidnapped them. Soon afterward, the girls were allegedly sighted and stopped in the streets of Cairo by a police officer, because one of them had a cross tattooed on her wrist (which many Copts have). The girls were wearing burqas; they told the policeman that they had converted to Islam and were seeking refuge at the home of a Muslim man because they feared their parents' anger. Following this, the girls reportedly turned themselves in to a police station, where a further investigation occurred into their disappearance. The girls supposedly maintained their story that they had left their families and converted to Islam of their own free will. They were put in a state care home during the investigation instead of being returned to their parents. The families' lawyer believed the girls were speaking under coercion.

EGYPT

According to law, underage girls cannot legally convert or marry of their own accord until they reach eighteen years of age, especially if they do not have ID cards, which are usually issued at age sixteen. Because Nancy and Christine Fathy were considered minors under the law, any conversion to Islam or subsequent marriage would not be recognized. Likewise, any perpetrators involved in the incident were liable to legal punishment.

Despite this, underage girls, as well as other Egyptian women, are still regularly victims of abduction by Muslim factions. Little is done by authorities to recognize what is really happening to these women and put a stop to it. Due to the frequency and gravity of this problem, Christian families in Egypt have been forced to relocate to new cities, or even to emigrate to another country to protect their daughters.

STORIES OF PERSECUTION

Hani

As a young man, Hani had tattooed a small cross on the inside of his wrist to show his pride in his Coptic Christian heritage. He had been born into a Christian family in Upper Egypt, and Hani himself was a bold, firm believer in Christ. People

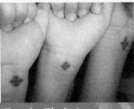

Coptic Christian cross tattoos

knew him to be kind, cheerful, and joyful; in fact his name in Arabic meant "joyful," an attitude he embraced and lived out in his daily life.

When he was of age, Hani joined the military for his required time of service. He soon discovered that as a Copt, he was a minority among the officers and soldiers. Before long his commanding officer and others began pressuring him to convert to Islam. They offered bribes of material wealth, but Hani was unmoved and held firm to his faith. The Muslim officers and soldiers then turned to more cruel and humiliating means of persuasion: they called Hani names, insisted he recite Quranic prayers, denied him food, beat him, and stomped on his back. He was provoked into fights and burned with cigarettes. His commanding officer would trip Hani, causing him to fall on his face, and then order the young Copt to lick his boots or to crawl on the floor.

Hani grew so humiliated and frustrated by this treatment that he warned his commanding officer that he would report him to military intelligence if it didn't stop. The commander threatened Hani in return, promising to "settle accounts" with him if he took such action. Hani then went on his family leave, and when it was over he returned obediently to his military service.

Only one week later Hani's family was called to identify his body at the local hospital. They were told that Hani had drowned in the Nile River, but a quick survey of his body told another story: one of torture and murder. To begin with, the tattooed cross on the inside of his wrist had been scraped off with a knife. His hands and feet had been burned, and his ribs and teeth had been broken. He also had stab wounds. His eyes were swollen, and his mouth was open with his tongue protruding as though he had been strangled. It was clear that Hani had not merely drowned.

Despite breaking his body, his attackers were unable to break his spirit or his faith. Hani remained steadfast even to his death, unwilling to let fear or intimidation dictate his life or cause him to deny the truth of Christ.

Samir

Just when he thought he had reached the pinnacle of his young Muslim life by earning a trip to the holy pilgrimage site of Mecca, "Samir" (not his real name) began having doubts about his religion. Samir had always been a well-respected Muslim and a top student of biochemistry at an Egyptian university. But at this time in his life, he felt it necessary to more deeply examine the beliefs of his faith and see how it compared with Christianity. He wanted to discover if Jesus Christ was real, and as a scientist decided to take an objective, scientific approach to the subject.

Samir began researching Christianity in a very practical way, including sneaking into churches to listen to sermons. Before long, Samir felt moved in his heart, and became convinced that Jesus was real and that He was the true Lord. He converted to Christianity, and almost immediately his parents kicked him out of their house. Samir was on his own, but that didn't deter him from desiring to be associated with Christ in every way. Within six months he decided to legally change the religion on his ID card from Muslim to Christian, though he must have known it was a dangerous step. When he attempted this, the public safety police instead arrested him—under the pretext of doing him a favor—and sent him to a mental hospital.

Samir could immediately tell that the doctors at the hospital were mostly radical Muslims, based on their long beards. They wasted no time in taking Samir away, punching him, and tying him up. He was physically subdued and forced to take various drugs, most of which were hallucinogenic. Every morning, afternoon, and evening the doctors made Samir take several pills. They also gave him injections and subjected him to electric shock therapy. Though he was given injections before the shock therapy to put him to sleep, Samir recalls two hands placing electrodes on him and voices telling him, "It's time for you to be shocked." Before long Samir lost control of his muscles and his mind diminished. His mouth hung open as he drooled.

After six weeks of "treatment," Samir was released from the hospital. His family was so ashamed of him that they would not take him in, and Samir had nowhere else to go. He tried finding sanctuary in churches, but many turned him away for fear of reprisal from authorities, who consider it a crime to help new Christian converts, especially those who have converted from Islam. Through The Voice of the Martyrs, Samir managed to get in touch with an evangelical pastor who helped Samir find a place to stay on his own.

Samir was institutionalized at least five more times in ten years. Each stay lasted about six weeks and consisted of the same treatment and torture, each visit leaving him more physically and mentally damaged. He has even been beaten and had teeth knocked out in the hospital, all in an attempt to turn him back to Islam. During one stay, however, Samir was given hope through the presence of two other Christians, with whom he had a chance to fellowship and pray. They even had a copy of the Bible, which they would read in order to find peace and encouragement amid the trouble and despair they faced. This gave Samir hope and courage for the future.

Samir has worked with a VOM-sponsored evangelist and gained some assistance since then, though as a Muslim-background believer in Egypt, he daily faces the threat of persecution and death for his faith. He gets regular phone calls from the public safety police to assure that he is not talking to others about Christianity. Samir remains firm, despite all he has been through, and though he faces physical and mental challenges due to the irreversible damage inflicted on him, he has a passion for helping blind and disabled Christians.

EGYPT

STRUCK DOWN BUT
NOT DESTROYED

*"We are hard pressed on every side, yet not
crushed; we are perplexed, but not in despair;
persecuted, but not forsaken; struck down,
but not destroyed—always carrying about
in the body the dying of the Lord Jesus,
that the life of Jesus also may be
manifested in our body."*

—2 CORINTHIANS 4:8–10

Persecution against Christians in Egypt happens not only to individuals, but to groups as well. As previous examples have shown, sometimes an entire community is attacked and terrorized at one time. In April 2011, thousands of Muslims stormed the Christian village of Minya, chanting, "There is no God but Allah, and Muhammad is his prophet!" They looted and burned houses as they streamed throughout the village. "Come outside!" they called out to the residents. "You are godless. You do not deserve to live; you do not worship a real god!" They dragged women from their houses and abused them.

Twenty-five-year-old Megad hid quietly inside his modest brick farmhouse, trying to protect his family, which consisted of his pregnant

107

young wife, his mother, and his two sisters. They were crying, and Megad grew more nervous as the Muslim extremists drew steadily closer to his house. He had noticed earlier when he arrived home from work that the men of the village were gone; the remaining unprotected women were being chased by a Muslim mob. He later learned that all the men had been arrested by security forces and taken to jail, which left the women alone and vulnerable. Megad described the entire incident as something from a horror movie.

This event occurred just after the start of the 2011 Revolution and a few days before Easter. Political upheavals and times of Christian celebration (such as during major holidays) are often catalysts for the worst outbreaks of persecution of Christians in Egypt. Law enforcement against the perpetrators is inadequate and inconsistent, sometimes nonexistent. Authorities often take little or no action to aid the Christian victims.

The Voice of the Martyrs works to help persecuted Christians in Egypt in various ways.

Due to fewer restrictions on building churches in Egypt than there used to be, a new church was being built in June 2013. A group of Muslims converged on the construction site with bulldozers and demanded that the building be torn down. Church buildings are particular targets for Muslim extremists, who wish to see Christianity in Egypt completely eliminated. Church bombings and burnings are frequent, leaving many Christians (or other bystanders) injured or killed. Christian bookstores are also attacked, and their merchandise destroyed. Because Bibles and other Christian literature are a deep source of comfort and consolation for the persecuted Christians of Egypt, VOM helps to sponsor a Christian bookstore, prints Christian literature for distribution in Egypt, and also provides Bibles through its Bibles Unbound program.

A Bible bookstore in Egypt

Farmer Saber Gadallah, an Egyptian Christian, had just worked fourteen hours in the field. As he sat down in his home to rest, there was a knock on the door. The teenage son of his Muslim neighbor wished to purchase some hay. Exhausted by his day's work, Saber sent his sixteen-year-old daughter out back to fetch the hay. The girl never returned. Another distinctive problem for Egyptian Christians is the kidnapping of young Christian girls, either Copts or Muslim-background believers, who are raped and/or forced to convert to Islam and marry Muslim men. To better protect their daughters, concerned Christian families often relocate, or they keep their daughters hidden away inside, terrified to let them go out on their own. VOM has helped sponsor safe houses for women—places where teenage girls can find protection from abduction and also experience spiritual encouragement and training.

Finally, Muslims who are interested in Christianity face being shunned and persecuted by their families, friends, and community if they persist in the study of Christianity or become Christians themselves. It is sometimes difficult for them to find a church in which to get help or sanctuary, and many new Muslim-background believers find themselves alone without recourse or aid. VOM helps provide job training and support to persecuted Muslim converts. These Chris-

EGYPT

tians also find instruction, guidance, peace, hope, and encouragement from their daily trials through television, radio, and Internet satellite broadcasts that are sponsored by VOM.

Political changes continue to occur within Egypt that may or may not prove beneficial to Egyptian Christians. Nearly a year after Morsi was forced out of office, Egypt elected its latest leader, Abdul Fattah al-Sisi, who was officially sworn in as president in June 2014. Formerly Egypt's army chief, al-Sisi had presided over the military ouster of Morsi and then immediately begun a campaign against the members and supporters of the Muslim Brotherhood, an operation which continues today. The new president's priorities focus on improving security (defeating terrorism in Egypt through eliminating the power and influence of the MB, which he declared a terrorist organization in December 2013) and enhancing the economy. "Throughout its extended history...our country has never witnessed a democratic peaceful handover of power," al-Sisi was quoted as saying in the *Daily Mail Reporter.* "The time has come to build a more stable future."

Christians are so far counting on their new president to make good his word, as their freedom and welfare within Egypt have been anything but stable. Many have shown their support of the man since Morsi's ouster, and are hopeful that

Abdul Fattah al-Sisi will bring positive change and renewal to Egypt. In an interview with *Time* Magazine just a few months before the elections, a prominent Christian businessman said, "If Egypt had not been saved by Sisi, you would have seen an exodus of all the Christians from Egypt." Some believers, however, feel that history could repeat itself if the president's strict policies become too authoritarian or if he fails to achieve his goals. The Muslim Brotherhood and other extremists could easily continue to target Christians for supporting him. After all, according to the previous interim president, Adly Mansour, who works very closely with al-Sisi and is supported by him, Egypt is still considered a Muslim state. The future welfare of Egypt's minority group, the Copts, and of other Egyptian Christians remains questionable.

Despite the earthly leaders who come to rule over the country, Egypt's decisive fate—and that of its Christian citizens—remains in the sovereign hands of the one true Lord and King, Jesus Christ. Believers in Egypt remain steadfast through political upheaval because of this fact. They have learned to ultimately place their trust not in political leaders, but in the God of heaven, who gives them strength and brings a definite purpose into their lives that provides peace in the midst of chaos, calm in the midst of the storm. They can claim, like the apostle Paul in his letter to the Corinthians, that they are "struck down, but not destroyed." Two millennia of political change and instability, which has trodden down Egyptian believers—maltreating, humiliating, and killing them—has not managed to destroy them. This is evidence of Christ's power in His Church, in the lives of His people in Egypt.

Believers around the world are urged to strengthen and uphold their Egyptian brothers and sisters through prayer.

FOR FURTHER READING

The following resources are a selection of those consulted in the writing of this book and are recommended for further reading. The Voice of the Martyrs and the author do not necessarily share all the views presented in these resources.

Books

Cannuyer, Christian. *Coptic Egypt: The Christians of the Nile*. New York: Harry N. Abrams, Inc. 2001.

Habib el Masri, Iris. *The Story of the Copts: The True Story of Christianity in Egypt*. Newberry Springs, CA: Saint Anthony Coptic Orthodox Monastery. 1982.

MacCulloch, Diarmaid. *Christianity: The First Three Thousand Years*. New York: Penguin Books. 2010.

Meinardus, Otto F. A. *Two Thousand Years of Coptic Christianity*. New York: The American University in Cairo Press. 1999.

Osman, Tarek. *Egypt on the Brink: From Nasser to Mubarak*. London: Yale University Press. 2011.

Partrick, Theodore Hall. *Traditional Egyptian Christianity: A History of the Coptic Orthodox Church*. Greensboro, NC: Fisher Park Press. 1996.

The Voice of the Martyrs. *Into the Den of Infidels: Our Search for the Truth.* Bartlesville, OK: Living Sacrifice Book Company. 2003.

Online Articles

BBC Staff. "Profile: Egypt's Muslim Brotherhood." *BBC News*. December 25, 2013.

Bohn, Lauren E. "Egypt's Christians Caught in Cross Fire." *Time*. August 26, 2013.

Chick, Kristen. "Across Egypt, Piles of Ash Where Church Pews Once Stood." *The Christian Science Monitor*. September 12, 2013.

CNN Staff. "Egypt Explained: 6 Key Questions." *CNN*. August 4, 2013.

Daily Mail Reporter Staff. "Egypt's Army Chief Sworn in as Leader…" *Mail Online*. June 9, 2014.

Goodenough, Patrick. "Egyptian Islamists Target Christian Churches in Wave of Apparently Coordinated Attacks." *CNS News*. August 15, 2013.

Lane, Gary. "Muslim Trafficking Networks Target Coptic Women." *CBN News*. October 10, 2012.

Martone, James. "Egypt's Christians Proud of History Traced to Jesus, Saint Mark." *Catholic Philly*. August 27, 2013.

Pinault, David. "Ready to be Martyrs." *America Magazine*. September 10, 2012.

Sirgany, Sarah and Laura Smith-Spark. "'Horrible': Christian Churches across Egypt Stormed, Torched." *CNN World News*. August 16, 2013.

Other Resources

The Voice of the Martyrs monthly newsletter and websites:

www.persecution.com (USA)
www.vomcanada.org (Canada)

Coptic Orthodox Church Network:
www.copticchurch.net

Open Doors: www.opendoors.org

RESOURCES

The Voice of the Martyrs has many books, videos, brochures, and other products to help you learn more about the persecuted church. In the US, to order materials or receive our free monthly newsletter, call (800) 747-0085 or write to:

The Voice of the Martyrs
P.O. Box 443
Bartlesville, OK 74005-0443
www.persecution.com
thevoice@vom-usa.org

If you are in Australia, Canada, New Zealand, South Africa, or the United Kingdom, contact:

Australia:
Voice of the Martyrs
P.O. Box 250
Lawson NSW 2783
Australia

Website: www.persecution.com.au
Email: thevoice@persecution.com.au

Canada:
Voice of the Martyrs, Inc.
P.O. Box 608
Streetsville, ON L5M 2C1
Canada

Website: www.vomcanada.org
Email: thevoice@vomcanada.org

New Zealand:
Voice of the Martyrs
P.O. Box 5482
Papanui, Christchurch 8542
New Zealand

Website: www.persecution.co.nz
Email: thevoice@persecution.co.nz

South Africa:
Christian Mission International
P.O. Box 7157
1417 Primrose Hill
South Africa

Email: cmi@icon.co.za

United Kingdom:
Release International
P.O. Box 54
Orpington BR5 9RT
United Kingdom

Website: www.releaseinternational.org
Email: info@releaseinternational.org

RESTRICTED NATIONS SERIES

Through the Restricted Nations series, learn about Christianity in the following countries, from the introduction of the gospel message until today, when Christians are persecuted for their faith. Weaving historical accounts with modern-day testimonies, these books will challenge you to share in the sufferings of Christians around the world and inspire you to pray for the persecuted Church today.

China

Colombia

Eritrea

India

Indonesia

Iran

North Korea

Pakistan

Sudan

Vietnam

To order these and other resources, visit www.VOMBooks.com

RESTRICTED NATIONS

China:
*The Blood-
Stained Trail*
(ISBN 978-0-
88264-029-7)

Colombia:
*The Gospel Invades
Enemy Territory*
(ISBN 978-0-
88264-033-4)

Eritrea:
*A People
Imprisoned*
(ISBN 978-0-
88264-028-0)

India:
*Tales of
Glory*
(ISBN 978-0-
88264-032-7)

Iran:
*Finding Hope in
the Axis of Evil*
(ISBN 978-0-
88264-031-0)

North Korea: *Good
News Reaches the
Hermit Kingdom*
(ISBN 978-0-
88264-030-3)

Pakistan:
*An Enduring
Witness*
(ISBN 978-0-
88264-034-1)

Sudan:
*Afflicted But
Not Forgotten*
(ISBN 978-0-
88264-026-6)

Vietnam:
*A Legacy of
Longsuffering*
(ISBN 978-0-
88264-035-8)

*To order these and other resources, visit
www.VOMBooks.com*